AMERICAN UNDERSTANDING OF INDIA: A SYMPOSIUM

American Understanding of India: A Symposium

Papers read at a conference held at the Library of Congress, 23-25 October 1986
Convened in conjunction with the Festival of India 1985-1986

Compiled and edited by
LOUIS A. JACOB

MANOHAR
2001

First published 2001

ISBN 81-7304-408-2

Published by
Ajay Kumar Jain for
Manohar Publishers & Distributors
4753/23 Ansari Road, Daryaganj
New Delhi 110002

Printed at
Rajkamal Electric Press
B 35/9 GT Karnal Road Indl Area
Delhi 110033

Contents

Preface

The Symposium on American Understanding of India took place at the Library of Congress during 23-25 October 1986. Sixteen scholars from the United States and India representing a variety of disciplines in the humanities and social sciences were invited to present papers. Two, Robert Crane and M.N. Srinivas, had been contributors to the beginnings of post-Independence scholarship on contemporary India. Others, Susanne Hoeber Rudolph, Burton Stein, Karl Potter, Joseph Elder, N. Gerald Barrier, A.K. Ramanujan and Charles White were in the generation of academic program builders in this country. Still others, Wendy O'Flaherty, Barbara Metcalf, Daniel Neuman, Barbara Stoler Miller and George Hart represent a new generation of mature American scholars researching and teaching Indian subjects.

The occasion for the symposium was the year and one-half Festival of India, 1985-86. Jointly sponsored by the governments of the United States and India, the Festival was a celebration of Indian culture for an American audience; an effort to enhance the image of India in American eyes. Museums such as the Metropolitan Museum of Art in New York, the National Gallery in Washington, the Cleveland Museum of Art, and the Asian Art Museum of San Francisco mounted major exhibits. Performances of classical Indian dance and music were presented at the Kennedy Center, the Lincoln Center and on university campuses and other stages throughout the country. Film festivals and craft shows toured extensively, and educational programs, academic conferences and symposia focused on numerous aspects of Indian life and Indian-American relationships. The annual summer folklife festival on the Mall in Washington, D.C. became an Indian fairground for a few days before and after 4 July, as Indian craftsmen and performers, brought to the Museum of Natural History for an extensive display called "Aditi: a festival of the living arts of India," transferred their activities out of doors.

The Symposium on American understanding of India was intended to present an opportunity for scholars and students of India to pause and look back at what they and their colleagues have contributed to an understanding of India, especially since World War II, and to consider how the community of South Asian scholars views the future for teaching and research. It also seemed important to discuss whether and how the fruits of that research might be made more generally available to the American public.

At a distance of forty years since the first South Asian area studies program was introduced at the University of Pennsylvania by W. Norman Brown, the symposium was also intended to provide an opportunity for a reassessment of the concept of area studies related to India and its neighbors and the achievements and failures of this type of approach during its period of ascendency. Problems concern the adequacy of teaching tools and whether researchers have an adequate opportunity to undertake necessary investigations, whether students are being required to meet the quality standards demanded of students of western cultures, whether student interest is sufficient to justify the teaching positions now in place and whether graduating students of South Asia can expect to find teaching opportunities available in their fields of interest. Much of the past of area studies has depended upon the infusion of extra-university funding from government and private sources, now much reduced and thought likely to come to an end. As this type of program nears completion of its first half-century, it is appropriate to reassess its accomplishments and to ask how and in what form it can and should continue.

Outside the college campus and its circle of scholars, popular knowledge of, interest in and attitudes toward India are not nearly so well informed as are those pertaining to more familiar European peoples. High school textbooks and other informational media usually devote little attention to South Asia and often tend to contribute to a negative perception of India and Indians. The diffusion as well as the discovery and transmission of knowledge and understanding has to be regarded as a continuing challenge to South Asianists and, as such, was also a concern of the symposium.

The symposium had a tripartite design. The first segment focused on American understanding of contemporary India; the second, our understanding of traditional India; and the third cultural interchange and American perceptions of Indian culture. Each segment was introduced by a major speaker who afterwards acted as moderator during briefer talks by four panel members representing a variety of disciplines. Each speaker was asked to emphasize the achievements of and prospects for American understanding of India in the context of his or her own speciality.

Two papers are presented here as major addresses concerned with traditional India. Karl Potter, who was initially invited to present the leading talk in this segment, fell ill suddenly and was unable to attend the conference. On very short notice, Wendy Doniger O'Flaherty kindly consented to speak in his stead. Her presence proved an enormous boon for the conference. Fortunately, Dr. Potter had submitted his paper well in advance and it is reproduced in this volume although it was not read during the sessions.

All presentations were revised and in one or two cases replaced by their authors for publication in this volume. The arrangement follows the order in which the talks were presented and then discussed. Unfortunately, the microphones were unable to pick up all of the discussion. Summaries are given of what was recorded.

There were many contributors to the symposium. Its realization was due primarily to the initiative of Asian Division Chief J. Thomas Rimer and the funding made available through Librarian of Congress Daniel J. Boorstin. Stanley Heginbotham and Richard Cronin of the Congressional Research Service worked with Louis Jacob and Allen Thrasher of the Southern Asian Section as principal planners, but many others in the Library contributed their services as consultants and assistants in various tasks. Alice Kniskern and Bruce Tapper served as advisors and Charles Stanhope monitored expenditures; Kim Moden and Nancy Mitchell coordinated use of the meeting site and service of life-sustaining food and coffee; Gene Roberts in the Exhibits Office supervised production of posters, programs and brochures; Nancy Shaffer of CRS was especially helpful in creating a conference mailing list which could be manipulated by computer; and John Husovsky of the Finance Office was helpful in expediting checks to the participants so they could pay their hotel bills. Ainslee Embree, A.K. Ramanujan and Ted Tanen visited Washington to participate in program planning. Stanley Heginbotham moderated the proceedings.

Section I

AMERICAN UNDERSTANDING OF CONTEMPORARY INDIA

American Perspectives on India: Voices in the Social Sciences

Susanne Hoeber Rudolph

I am delighted that the Library of Congress has decided to assemble us here, at one of the last, capping and summary events of the Festival of India. All India scholars have incurred a great debt to the Library over the decades since Indian independence. It has provided important leadership in the era marked by the PL480 library acquisitions program, by collecting magnificently and by directing a Delhi office that organized the enormous task of transmitting India's prolific literary output to the South Asia libraries here. We are all grateful to the Library, to its Asian division, and Tom Rimer, and to our colleagues of the South Asia Section, Lou Jacob, Stanley Heginbotham, Allen Thrasher—longtime colleagues and co-workers in the stacks and bookshelves of life.

I have been asked to tell you this evening what the American social scientists have contributed to the understanding of India since independence in 1947. That is a mammoth task, given the industriousness of that small community of social scientists. In recent weeks, I found myself drowning in a veritable sea of articles and books, and have only recently bubbled to the surface to tell you what I found. One happy aspect of this task is that Indian independence indeed provides a watershed and is succeeded by a time of new beginnings.

The American social scientists that went to India in the 1950s thought that the world—both the world of the social sciences and the world of Indian scholarship—had just been born. They were exhilarated to be in on the delivery. American colleges and universities were quite innocent of knowledge about India, bar a few Sanskritists, and bar a few historians of the Commonwealth. They were helped by the fact that British scholarship on India stood in the shadow of its colonial provenance, suspect as the ideology of imperialism. American scholarship was sure it had no political motives. Its only motives were truth and rigor. Our Indian colleagues too thought it a time of beginnings. They were mostly midnight's children, to use Salman Rushdie's metaphor, born or grown up after midnight of 15 August 1947, and they were in the process of reinventing their own scholarship. We were all invited to write on a *tabula rasa*, to devise new ways of seeing. We did not have to contend with a complex, elaborately built, prior tradition of scholarship to which we might at best add an incremental modification of theory or of fact. We could shape paradigms, imprint the field. We could invent India.

The historical environment that nourished social science scholarship was also newborn: India became independent. The United States as a polity had to deal with India face to face, not via the British ally. American scholars had to deal with Indian scholars directly, face to face, or article to article. There was a sense of rebirth in American social sciences. The post-war generation of social science graduate students was launched on a devout mission: to sweep away the aging, institutional, intellectualist, and normatively oriented approaches of the pre-war period, and to install one or another of the fresh new approaches to reality—structural functionalism in sociology; behavioralism in political science; the search for indigenous categories in anthropology; the search for underprivileged data and understudied classes in history; political economy in all the social sciences. And finally there was a new birth in social science in India, as Indian scholars burst the boundaries of colonial scholarship, supported by the expansion of post-graduate education in the social sciences.

As I began to write this essay, I encountered an elemental problem. What is social science? So that I would be sure to have a sound indigenous formulation of my categories I inquired what the Indian Council of Social Science Research thought social science was. The ICSSR had a set of categories. They excluded history. I decided that had a lot more to do with the somewhat accidental history of bureaucratic politics in India (The Indian Council of Historical Research "does" history) than with a fundamental intellectual decision. I looked next at suggestive bibliographies, since, as you well know at LC, bibliographers are the lords of categorization. I found that Maureen Patterson and Bill Alspaugh were such committed, cross-disciplinary Chicagoans that they didn't pay a lot of attention to discipline when they organized their mammoth bibliography of South Asia. And Jerry Barrier's recent bibliography for the Festival of India, which does use disciplines to an extent, thought history and social sciences were separate categories and didn't think political science was a category within social science.

I propose to organize my remarks today mainly by reference to history, anthropology and political science. This is not because geography and sociology have not played a part, they have—how, in the era of Joseph Schwartzberg's *Atlas* could any of us forget it? Economics has paid rather little attention to India. That is because economics has reached such a splendid level of universalism that mere concrete cultures and civilizations no longer impinge upon it. Those who did pay attention (Bhagwati, Desai, Bardhan, Veit, Rosen, among others) had to leave the ranks of the math modelers. While doing so, I will look mainly at these disciplines because they allow me to make some generalizations about the social sciences in general.

One more disclaimer. I discovered early on in preparing these remarks that I needed to mention names, to evoke a disciplinary turn here, an innovation there. It is a hurtful business, because some of those choices are random, and each name excludes some others that I value equally. To be inclusive would be even worse; it would bore you. So I place the onus for my choices on the wish of my audience not to be overwhelmed by inclusiveness.

Of course there is the continuing question to what extent American social science scholarship will continue to have access to India. The government of India has always been nervous about certain categories dear to the heart of the social scientist: ethnic and religious studies; studies out on sensitive frontiers where interesting tribes might be found; studies of regions where there is significant dissent. Most of us respect these areas of sensitivity. But there are also more elusive principles of exclusion, and discovering these principles has itself become an interesting social science. Some weeks ago the American Institute of Indian Studies Executive Board spent at least ten minutes trying to deduce, as good social scientists might, the categories of exclusion from the actual exclusions.

My own interpretation is that we Americans have been only too normalized into the Indian scene. *India Today*, some weeks ago, carried a story in which it showed that an Indian businessman could expect to wait 14 months for his license application to be cleared. Most AIIS fellows did better than that, but this year one-quarter of AIIS fellows were not yet cleared 16 months after their applications. Perhaps this practice has a positive aspect. American scholars are prematurely graduated into the Vanaprashta stage, the stage of the holy forest dwellers of the ancient texts. Having rented their houses and given up their teaching jobs and their salaries, they huddle in forest cottages and live on the herbs and fruits of the marsh and meadow. Thus the process of assimilation to indigenous categories proceeds apace. And the study of Indian bureaucracy, which too few of us pursue, is actually advanced by our own experience.

My story today has to do with what the American social scientists did after independence. Over the last 40 years, they created a voice for themselves, or rather, voices. Those voices rose out of a complex social process and out of the interaction of numerous social forces; one was the intellectual traditions of particular disciplines in America and Europe; another was the American political and cultural environment, including America's power relationship to other countries in a world system; and finally, the nature of Indian intellectual and scholarly innovation over four decades. In short, American disciplines, America's power position and Indian scholarship shaped the Americans.

There were two dimensions to finding a voice, a methodological and a normative one. Methodology meant having to define what should count as data, what was reality. For some the issue was whether there was any reality at all. A normative orientation meant positioning one's self between dispassionate and polemical, accepting and critical, neutral and committed—and, if committed, to what and to whom.

In the normative sphere Indians and Americans set agendas for themselves, influenced each other and revised each other's agendas. Just after "midnight," the easiest part for Americans in acquiring a voice was to oppose imperialism. Americans valued Woodrow Wilson, Franklin Delano Roosevelt, self-determination and a world that was made safe for democracy—by Americans. Nationalism was a positive force. It had freed India. There was not the slightest doubt or ambivalence that the American voice would ally itself with a free and democratic India. The waning imperial voices of the British Tory fringe had in the 1950s no such support as they have in the America of the 1980s, where neo-conservative romance about the British Empire colors the edges even of academic studies. And Indians supported Americans in their self-definition as opponents of imperialism. In the halcyon days before the discovery of neo-imperialism there was a happy receptivity to American social scientists. If there were conflicts—and there were—some thought them merely a matter of bad vibes between Morris Opler and D.N. Majumdar, perhaps a matter of contrasting cultural styles in academic behavior. No one thought such conflict a structural question rooted in more fundamental aspects of American and Indian power relations. The problem of acquiring a normative voice was eased by the fact that Americans liked studying democracies and pluralist patterns of politics, and India had both in abundance. The Indian "project," to create a modern economy and a redistributional polity, appealed to Americans. The American academic establishment, unlike the Washington establishment, thought socialism might be a good thing.

But the matter of acquiring a voice soon became more complex. The voices of social scientists began to sort themselves out into two very different musical patterns. On the one hand was the sanguine voice of those who stressed the adaptive and incremental patterns in Indian society and polity, who thought the old society had within it the means of its own regeneration. On the other hand could be heard the voice of the more critical and/or pessimistic observers who focused on underlying cleavages and conflicts, imagining Indian underclasses on the edge of revolt.

These divergent voices constructed different Indias. One was an India in which change was and would be a process accomplished without tearing the web of society. "People throughout India commonly keep to traditional social patterns while adapting themselves to modern circumstances," wrote David Mandelbaum in *Society in India*, 1971 (p. 655), speaking for a broadly shared view that change in India was adaptive. When Lloyd Rudolph and I entitled our book, in 1967, *The Modernity of Tradition*, we meant to convey that India was likely to change by modifying the idioms and structures of its own civilization rather than by abandoning them and substituting others. We were certainly part of the "Chicago School" in creating such a vision, but the vision was widely shared. Joe Elder, writing his Ph.D. thesis within the very bosom of Parsonian polarities, in which the achieved would displace the ascribed and the impersonal the affective, declared that U.P. factory workers regularly combined the pattern variables. Milton Singer's semiotic variant is only the most recent version of such a perspective: "The activities of reinterpreting and restructuring old signs and symbols of Indian identity are the activities of growing and changing selves" (*Man's Glassy Essence*, p.187, Bloomington, Indiana University Press, 1984).

Not only American but also Indian voices divided into these two streams. Most of the scholars at the Center for the Study of Developing Societies in Delhi shared a vision of an India which would adapt its institutions and values to create a new polity and society (Kothari, Nandy, Roy, Ahmed, Krishna, Sethi, Shah). India would not experience total revolution. It would experience, as Rajni Kothari put it, incremental revolution (*Politics in India*, New Delhi and New York, 1970).

Other Indian voices, many of them in the pages of *Economic and Political Weekly*, disagreed. They saw the stress on adaptation within the formulas and structures of Indian civilization as an American version of Brahmanical mystification. The Indians who saw conflict rather than adaptation as the road to the future were often neo-Marxians. The Americans, with a few exceptions, sprang rather from egalitarian and populist stock.

Robert Miller, an anthropologist who wrote on Indian untouchables, thought he saw an alliance between the caste system in Indian culture and a caste system in American academia. He said that those who spoke of India's Great Tradition, the overarching high culture created by Brahmanic Hinduism, spoke as if that tradition were relevant for all Indians; they failed to recognize that it was disowned by India's underclasses. The article, "Button, Button, Great Tradition, Little Tradition, Whose Tradition?" in effect accused the Chicagoans of neo-Brahmanism, and called for a sort of academic anti-Brahman movement (*Anthropological Quarterly*, 39, 1966). Kathleen Gough, Joan Menscher, Eleanor Zelliot, Owen Lynch, Francine Frankel, speaking with quite different degrees of intensity and from different theoretical assumptions, considered the argument for adaptability of traditional institutions as a defense of inherited power structures.

The accusation that we were defending an old order came as a surprise to the theorists of cultural evolution and adaptation, among whom I would count myself and Lloyd Rudolph. We were positioned to fight on an altogether different front, and against a different opponent. We had before us a large body of sociological literature, including Seymour Martin Lipset's *The First New Nation*, and his "The Requisites of Democracy;" Daniel Lerner's *Modernizing the Middle East*; and the early volumes produced by the Comparative Politics Committee of the Social Science Research Council. All of these were in various ways colored by Talcott Parsons' construction of the European and the non-European world, by the pattern variables that allowed one unmistakably to comprehend the qualities necessary to enter the modern era. These were the vanguard ideologists of American post-war social science; they were infected by the notion that America would show the world its future. The values and structures of the old societies were both obsolete and wrong-headed. Political, sociological and economic development required family structures, social functions, character features and ideologies that were scarce in Asia—including India. Only a total remodelling of these features, a replacement of old structures by new, of old persons by new, would allow the world of Asia to improve the economic and political conditions of its people.

The line of argument had a curious and paradoxical aspect: it was a call for total cultural revolution issued by conservative Americans to socialist Indians led by a mildly radical Fabian, Jawaharlal Nehru. The call implied that nothing less than the total divestment of previous forms and ideologies, a total war against the old culture, from the joint family through caste through "fatalism," would permit India to enter the modern age.

It seemed to many of us that such an evaluation of the nature of Indian society, and such a project for change, was ethnocentric. When we emphasized adaptation, we did so as part of an explicit denial and rejection of the presumptions of development theory. India did not have to divest itself of its character, culture and social structures. These were sufficiently various internally that some would serve as links to the modern era, and would prove adaptable in surprising ways.

Lloyd Rudolph and I, for example, hung our own argument on the question of caste and politics. We said caste in the context of universal franchise would prove to be anti-caste. The solidarity of large numbers of individual lower castes would prove a threat to the hierarchical structure of the caste system. The horizontal ties of caste members to each other would undermine the vertical dependence of individual caste members on higher caste patrons. A traditional institution, caste, would acquire a more egalitarian face in the new era (*The Modernity of Tradition*).

Our first trip to India, in 1956-57, confirmed Lloyd and myself in such a perspective. For many of us, it was the experience of sloshing around in the data, of living in the society, that lifted the myths of development theory. That year, in Rajasthan and Madras, we watched two variants of the *ancien régime*, the Rajput rulers of princely Rajasthan, and the Brahmanic establishment in Madras, work out their response to the challenge of democracy. It was the time of the second general election, and it had become apparent to both orders that universal franchise was here to stay. New forces had grasped the levers of elections to push them aside. In Rajasthan, a Rajput noble order that cherished its aristocratic and chivalric codes, learned swiftly to bargain with populist politicians and to adapt to commercial values when it would do them good. In Madras, the prediction that Brahmanic fastidiousness concerning the lower castes or the other-worldliness of their philosophic/religious orientations would deter adaptation was swamped by the energetic efforts of a portion of Tamil Brahmans to find new roles in a mass society with new technology. Andre Beteille saw alliances in Tamil villages between Brahmans and Untouchables against middle castes; Milton Singer witnessed the successful move of Tamil Brahmans into business as the anti-Brahman movement blocked the entrance for Brahmans into bureaucracy and higher education. Adaptation was swift and dramatic.

Nor was adaptation a game at the end of which the same social structure emerged in a new form. Both Brahmans and Rajputs significantly lost power—but not all power. New rural and urban classes gained power—but not all classes and not all equally. We witnessed the first steps, not of a revolution, but of an incremental revolution, to use Rajni Kothari's phrase. It was a revolution in which old cultural skills and structures were reshaped rather than trashed.

This line of argument was directed against the ethnocentrism of development theory. But it left our left flank exposed to those critics for whom adaptation was too limited an agenda. Adaptation was not revolution. The Rajput order may have been diminished, but it was not driven out of politics or the landed economy, Daniel Thorner argued. The lower castes rose in politics, but only their powerful and prosperous did, not their poor and oppressed, Francine Frankel argued. Adaptation, so rose an entire chorus from *Economic and Political Weekly*, was not "systemic change." These divergent normative voices persist among both American and Indian social scientists.

The second arena in which Americans sought to develop a distinctive voice for their scholarship was the methodological dimension. Here Americans became identified with a revolt against formalism. Two Indian scholars, writing for the ICSSR review of literature, said: "From the sixties onwards, one notices a conscious realization that the 'substance' of politics can differ from its 'form' and consequently there has been a trend away from formal description toward a more incisive treatment of the institutional infrastructures and the substantive processes" (M.R. Deshpande and N.G.S. Kini, "Studies on Institutions of Parliamentary Democracy," in ICSSR, *A Survey of Research on Political Science*, Vol. 1, *Political System*, Allied, New Delhi, 1979, p. 48). They were right. There was a shift from form to substance in all the social sciences.

The revolt against formalism meant something different in history, in anthropology and in political science, but in all three there was some sort of revolt. In each case the revolt was related to a reevaluation of what was respectable or "real" evidence, what were appropriate sources. The effect of new sources on social sciences has parallels to the effect of new instrumentation on the physical sciences. A new lens brings into view new galaxies that enforce a shift of theory and of emphasis.

This purely methodological revolution was not just a matter of research technologies. It had a normative dimension. Scholars searched out underprivileged data, and they did so because they were documenting and explaining the fate of underprivileged social categories—lower classes, lower castes, ignored genders (women), ignored political categories (regions). In a general way, new sources and the increase in what are called "subaltern" studies, studies of the noncommissioned officers of society, went side-by-side.

For the historians, the revolt against formalism occasioned a re-assessment of the relative worth of documentation in the India Office Library in London or the National Archives at Delhi as against other less elite sources. The London and Delhi archives implied a certain view of reality: the real action was the decisions of the Viceroy, the Executive Council, the Secretary of State for India at London whose memorials filled the great imperial archives. Different data could be found in the District Collectorate, in the godown behind the servants' quarters. The scholar who went out with his dustcloth, his microfilm camera, and the help of a superannuated but knowledgeable peon, had to untie legal size bundles to make his way to the new reality. Such archives implied that more real reality could be found by shifting research downwards in the social and political structure and outward from the metropolis and its institutions. The lens focussed on the district, the mofussil, regional and local power structures and lower levels of administration. Such new sources reflected a more general egalitarian thrust in social history. If George in France constructed a less bloodthirsty image of French revolutionary crowds by finding their rather solid social background and motives in hospital records and personal ledgers, India scholars would find a revised history in the districts.

Employing such new forms of data and a countercyclical suspicion of old truths, scholars such as Bernard Cohn and Robert Frykenberg, working in different record offices in north and south, thought they discovered that India in the 1830s was not governed from London or Delhi at all. It was not governed by the Viceroy, or the Legislative Councils and the ICS. It was governed by the tehsildars and clerks that kept the files and knew the social networks. If the *raj* thought to impose a revenue policy or tenancy regulation, it had to reckon with the diversionary skills of the landed classes and their connections into the lower levels of the secretariat.

The thrust of this writing was not merely to change the locale of action, but to challenge the ideologies in terms of which elites justify their hegemony. It meshed with the anti-imperialist preferences of American social scientists. The new Americans and their new sources said that the Englishman and ex-civil servant Philip Mason was wrong to believe that the Indian Civil Service was a morally driven status group. He was wrong to believe that the ICS fit comfortably into the paternalistic role of local ruler. He was wrong to believe it was engaged in an intimate and warmly personalistic pursuit of duty. Most civil servants served not as paternalistic collectors but as impersonal figures in the secretariats that no peasant ever penetrated. They were selected less by merit than by dynastic succession; the ICS ran in families. They knew so little about the power structures over which they presided that clever, ambitious Indians and subalterns could maneuver the outcomes, and enrich themselves and *de facto* run the system. These insights were in line with the anti-formalist strain among organization theorists in America and Europe. Organizations were not run from the top; they were run from the bottom, by the petty office and shop floor functionaries that populate them.

Among students of nationalism, both political scientists and historians, the revolt against formalism had yet a different meaning. It meant turning eyes away from the seductive but ultimately obfuscating ideologies and ideals of Tilak, Gokhale, Nehru and Gandhi to the true substructure of material and power interests, locally situated. The most powerful thrust came from the neo-Namierites at Cambridge (England). For Sir Lewis Namier there were no Whig politics, no ideals, no values. There were just the idealists' gloss on real interests. Real interests could be found by looking at local economic and social power holders and factions. The Cambridge School of India historians transferred much of this perspective to India (without reading sympathetically Herbert Butterfield's response to Namier). There it elaborated a sort of Burton-Turton view of nationalism. When Turton (or is it Burton?), the English collector in *Passage to India*, watches the Indians whom he had invited to his garden party, he says: "We know why he's here, I think—over that contract ... and he's the astrologer who wants to dodge the municipal building regulations ..." It was an anti-idealist perspective that appealed to scholars for whom the idealizing versions of Gandhi, Nehru and the nationalist movement seemed both soft and insufficiently specified.

One aspect of the shift from the "formal" aspects of nationalism was a shift from center to periphery, from the unified national movement to the components out of which it had been built. This led American social scientists to recognize the diversity of forces that led nationalism, and the significance of the dissenting themes. The American Bengalis such as John Broomfield and Leonard Gordon discovered that Bengal's view of Gandhi, the Gujarati bania, was colored by the bhadralok's inhospitable view of Marwari merchants. It was colored too by enthusiasm for Subhas Chandra Bose's militant nationalism. At the same time these scholars showed how Bengal invented, in 1905, many of the themes—for example Swadeshi—that entered Gandhi's portfolio of tactics. The American Tamils (Irschick, Hardgrave, Waghorne, Barnett) discovered that the anti-Brahman movement in Madras was deterred by the leadership of the Madras Congress. They discovered also how Tamil Nadu built its own variant of cultural politics from 1920 to 1980, and how Tamil institutions took a distinctive form (Appadurai, Presler, Breckenridge). The American Punjabis (Jones, Wallace, Heeger, Barrier, Jurgensmeyer, Heimsath, Ramusack) stressed how the organized Hindu reformers of the Arya Samaj fed into the Punjabi variant of nationalism.

But let me return to the theme of revolt against formalism, and say a word about its implications for Political Science. Political Science was washed over by a heavy wave of behaviorism in the 1960s. Most political scientists of my generation have gone through a reaction against it. We reacted against behaviorism's claim to scientific neutrality by saying that social science neither could nor should be value-neutral. We should specify our norms and allow them to invigorate our social science. But that was not the most central aspect of the behavioral revolution as it arrived in India.

American behaviorism in the 1960s had two faces. One face was its purely technical, mechanical aspect, embodying new research technologies that gave it the appearance of scientific rigor. The other face was its role as unmasker of spurious realities. Formal institutions, proclaimed policies, promulgated law; all of these were declared to be mere pious intentions, cardboard institutions. A rigorous attention to actual behavior would reveal them as the empty shells they were.

The technology of behaviorism led to counting. It generated quantifiable data by means of questionnaires that were thought to elicit attitudes. It did so by means of assembling aggregate data on the social background of legislators, civil servants, businessmen, party members and voters. In the Indian context, the technologies of behaviorism received great impetus from the conduct of elections at the national, state and panchayat level. Both Indians and Americans used the investigative technology to probe new problems of participatory democracy. Alliances between Indian and American social scientists produced an international study of values. Alliances between the Survey Research Center at the University of Michigan, the Center for the Study of Developing Societies, Eric Da Costa's Institute of Public Opinion and yet others generated studies of electoral behavior.

Almost everybody got into the game of electoral studies and survey research: Weiner, Field, Eldersveld, Bjorkman, Marvik, Bashir, Ahmed, Rajni Kothari, Ramesh Roy, Richard Sisson, Daniel Graves, Harold Gould, William Vanderboek, Biplab Das Gupta, W.H. Morris-Jones (to mention only some of the most obvious). It was an industry that generated a generation of Ph.D. theses both here and there. Some theses were mindless duplications of a fashionable technology that allowed the author to show the marks of industriousness while avoiding concepts. It eased the life of the thesis director: go to the field, young man, administer 150 questionnaires, make some tables, and you will get a Ph.D. It encouraged the transfer of "items" tested in American cultural contexts without inquiring what cultural and historical experience had made those questions meaningful in the U.S.A. Some investigations, however, revealed the unexpected or confirmed the expected—e.g., it was both expected and worthwhile to know that the Brahmans and Rajput landlords—the old classes—did well in the new round of panchayati raj in Rajasthan (thus Iqbal Narain, P.C. Mathur, S.P. Varma); it was important to learn how minority voting (by tribals, untouchables) diverged (Weiner, Field); and how regional trends washed out at the national level (Das Gupta and Morris-Jones). And it was this research, during its brief heyday in the late 1960s, which yielded the most important instances of genuine collaboration between Indian and overseas social scientists—thus Verba and Bhatt; Ahmed and Eldersveld; Morris-Jones and Das Gupta.

There is the other face of behaviorism, the one it shows when it acts as an unmasker of spurious realities. Empiricism is generally seen as a thoroughly unrevolutionary force. But that is partly wrong. Empiricism, like scientific materialism, is suspicious of proclaimed ideals; of promulgated law; of the intended consequences of formal institutions—courts, parliaments, administration. It suspects a divergence between ostensible and actual, between declared motive and real interest, between intent and reality. It has in common with scientific materialism the wish to show that laws have unanticipated effects, and institutions serve purposes the reverse of what they claim. What behaviorism lacks, of course, is a theory, such as class interest, that explains the difference between the declared motive and the real outcome.

Never mind that it has no such theory. In India in the 1950s and 60s, behaviorism joined the war against formalism. The phenomenon is noticeable, for example, in the study of the law. Indian legal studies have been the monopoly of lawyers, and their subject matter has been the logic of precedent and the framework of the text. Constitutional studies followed suit. There was virtually no attention to judicial behavior. Judges were reasoning animals, not political or social creatures. They were not affected by their social or economic status, let alone by political motives.

The spirit in which law and the constitution were read in India suggested a certain Brahman reverence for sacred texts without the great flexibility the Brahman legalists showed in shaping or adapting Dharmasastra. A young Indian woman who heard one of my lectures on caste in India in 1960 told me, "There is no longer any caste; the Indian constitution has abolished untouchability." Among some scholars, the word was as good as the deed, indeed, the written word was better than the deed. Behaviorism in legal studies carried on by Marc Galanter, George Gadbois, Upendra Baxi, R.K. Dhavan and others sought to show the actual as against the intended consequences of legislation.

Marc Galanter, the product of a new direction in American legal studies that brought social science inquiry to bear on the shaping of the law, on the behavior of the justices, and the impact on citizens, spent 20 years looking at the meaning of India's unique constitutional protection of the underprivileged. His work was the result of an effort to study society and law or law in society. George Gadbois investigated the background and preferences of justices. They took heart eventually from a new generation of Indian writers who sought to break the formal mold of legal and constitutional studies—Upendra Baxi, R.K. Dhavan and others—who sought to understand courts as embedded in a political and historical climate.

For other political scientists the revolt against formalism took the form of moving from the capital to the states, from the state capital to the district, following an implicit hypothesis that power had moved downward and to the periphery. Gandhi and Nehru, the working committee of the Congress party, its parliamentary board, the sort of thing Stanley Kochanek and I used to do, these seemed more and more the merely formal aspects of political processes (the more so when they fell into decay in Mrs. Gandhi's era). The real levers of socio-political change lay in the district and the tehsil, the local cooperative and the panchayat. That is where the American social scientists were now to be found: Brass, Weiner, Franda, Heginbotham, Taub, Januzzi, Rosenthal, Elliott, Manor. The march to the districts was led by an early volume on leadership edited by Richard Park and Irene Tinker, that assembled the vanguard writers of the new local *genre*. The challenge was to show how the formal party or administrative structures were built out of the local power coalitions; how these in turn related to changing local economic and status interests; and how coalitions had to change if new interests were to be represented.

The last methodological wave I would mention is one that is once more explicitly concerned with values, the emphasis on political economy. Political economy did not migrate to India as quickly as it did to Latin

America, where it arrived via dependency theory. Dependency theory, an important counterpoint to development theory, did not succeed so well in India. That is in part because dependency theory sees the impact of international economic and political forces as central to the explanation of growth and stagnation in Third World countries. The hypothesis works better for the countries of Latin America or Africa, heavily dependent on foreign export/import, investment, loans and aid than it does in India. India, in consequence of deliberate policy choices, is relatively less dependent on foreign powers on all those dimensions. But the concern with class, economic structures, with the notion that economy shapes polity, all of which are an element in dependency theory, did migrate into the social science studies of India.

Much of the impetus for political economy was Indian. The agendas for studying political economy were written more by Indian economists than by political scientists, as many of them outside as inside the university. Indian economists concerned with social policy have been far more institutionally mobile than Indian political scientists: they can be found in research institutes like the Gokhale Institute for Politics and Economics, in the Planning Commission, in the Indian Statistical Institute, in the World Bank, and in the many institutions founded by the Indian Council of Social Science Research. These economists in turn had special forums for their work—*Economic and Political Weekly*; *Seminar*; *Mainstream*. Such journals, in the hands of editors such as Krishna Raj, Romesh and Raj Thapar, encouraged a combination of theoretical, normative and empirical concerns. They encouraged a degree of appropriate relevance not general for professional economic journals. It is this complex of Indian policy-oriented economists, Indian research institutions and intermediate level journals, that wrote the agenda for many American political scientists in the seventies and eighties. Americans such as Francine Frankel, Subiah Kannapan, Terry Neale, George Rosen and Pranab Bardhan had already turned to political economy questions in the early 1970s, following earlier historical work by Morris Morris. Economists from the Harvard Advisory Group and others addressed India's problems—Papanek, Mason, Weiskopf, Marglin, Kenneth Galbraith, as ambassador and economist, attended to the Indian economy; so did Veit, Mellor and others. But they were followed by a whole new generation of political economists, including Herring, Attwood, Bouton, Gent, Baruah, Kohli, McAlpin, Ludden, and others in politics, history and anthropology. If electoral studies produced the largest number of genuine collaborations between Indians and Americans, political economy emerged as the arena in which Americans learned most significantly from Indians.

Anthropology has been disproportionately important in American scholarship on India. This phenomenon was viewed with some dismay by Indians, who recognized anthropology as the study of the primitive by the civilized, as something Verrier Elwin did to the tribes of the northeast frontier areas or Meyer Fortes to the West African tribes, or D.N. Majumdar to the Ho or the Khasa. Much of the anthropology practiced in India until the war was the anthropology of preliterate people living in social isolates. It conceived of villages or tribes as self-contained units whose internal structure and values were relatively unaffected by the external forces of economy, polity and cultural diffusion.

The anthropology that Americans developed after World War II spoke in a different voice. Just before and during the war, anthropology had come home, that is, had turned from "primitive" isolates to complex, literate, national and sub-continental cultures. The American anthropologists in the course of World War II had been asked to explain Japanese culture to Americans who did not understand it (Ruth Benedict), or American culture to Americans who needed to become self-conscious about it (Margaret Mead). National character studies sought to grasp whole civilizations, their mythic structures, their family types, their social relations, their ideological unities. While eventually repudiated as the unnatural child of social psychology and anthropology, these studies were one element in the coming home of anthropology to complex civilization. Another was the growth of urban ethnology within America, practiced in sociology departments more than anthropology departments, both agreeing on a rough division of labor that assigned cities to sociologists and villages to anthropologists. The Lynds' study of Middletown was part of such a homecoming. (Parenthetically, urban sociology never developed very much among Americans looking at India. With the exception of Lambert's, Elder's, Morris's, and Taub's studies, urban and industrial forces have not received much attention.)

The mingling of theory that addressed macro social structures with theory and ethnography that addressed micro structures occurred in several places, affecting the nature of anthropology: Talcott Parsons, macro-Weberian in the Harvard Department of Social Relations in the 1950s, infiltrated psychology and anthropology with theories that forced consideration of the micro community in the context of the civilization of which it was a part. Robert Redfield of Chicago concurrently led a generation to consider the village—in Mexico, in India—as imbedded within its civilization. My colleagues Milton Singer, Bernard Cohn and McKim Marriott spoke of Great and Little traditions in India. This was a posing of the issue that licensed anthropologists to pay attention to the local as well as the universal, to the non-literate and oral as well as the textual, and to look at family, caste, temple, weddings, festivals and all those phenomena Milton Singer called "cultural performances."

By the time the first post-war generation of anthropologists went to India, they were ready to recognize Indian villages were not the isolates Henry Mayne and several generations of civil servant/scholars had believed them to be. They were ready to understand the village in the context of the classical texts and macro structure of Indian civilization, to recognize the culture of the illiterates they studied as a component of a literate civilization.

There were Indian colleagues whose perspectives were congenial to this integrated vision of Indian folk culture and high culture, a vision that led away from the village and to the cities, or from the village to the region. Nirmal Kumar Bose, Irawati Karve, M.N. Srinivas, Surajit Sinha and L.P. Vidyarthi conceived of anthropology in a new vein that in many ways paralleled that of the Americans. Karve's work showed the overlap between Dravidian language and culture zones on the one hand and Dravidian kinship patterns on the other. These contrasted with Indo-Aryan language zones and kinship patterns. Her vision was grounded in a perception that forces beyond ethnographic isolates were crucial in cultural processes. So was Bose's presumption of a material base distinguishing cultural areas.

The most important interlacing between Indian and American anthropological insights of that time arose out of the work of M.N. Srinivas, who is here today to help us close the circle. His conceptions of Sanskritization and Westernization provided a parallel theoretical framework to the macro perspective on local institutions that the Americans used.

Anthropology like the other social sciences was affected by the behavioral revolution, and had to work out its own response to the ethnocentric bias in development theory. The behaviorist enthusiasm was brief but sharp. It was all very well for M.N. Srinivas to say that mobile castes would Sanskritize, would adopt the rituals and dress and deities and customs of higher castes, and for all the rest of us to believe him. It might even be true. But did it mean anything? If a low caste person donned a sacred thread, became a vegetarian and forbade his widowed sister to remarry, would he succeed in mystifying his fellow villagers into new kinds of treatment? McKim Marriott's painstaking studies of interactive behavior—photographs and charts of who sits where on the charpoy; who sits next to whom; who takes kaccha and who pucca food from whose hands—represented an empiricist cut at the merely ideological superstructure of Sanskritization.

But while this phase added important modifications to previous generalizations it was soon succeeded by another methodological preoccupation. Anthropology developed its own specific reaction against the ethnocentric face of development theory. To be sure, by its built-in propensity to cultural relativism, anthropology was in any case better equipped to see the world through the lens of the native. But now it turned to ethnosociology, a sociology written, as it were, by Manu, and ethnopsychology, a psychology derived from what were thought to be indigenous conceptions of the person (Marriott). Ethnosciences are as two-faced as was behaviorism, correcting previous narrowness, creating new narrowness. They forbid the kind of externality of perspective by which the perceiving eye, schooled, for example, in post-enlightenment rationalism, viewed the kisan's rituals of fructification either as false science or as a naive rationality disguising itself in flossy ceremonial (raheja). They insist that the native construction be taken exactly for what it is, that the perceiving eye and the native eye become one. It calls for a sort of ascetic leaving behind of the mental goods, of the conceptual schemes one has acquired in the course of an Anglo-American education. Instead, one is to clothe oneself in the native constructions provided 'by the astrologer, the vaid, the temple healer, the woman over her *chulha*, the marriage broker, the scientists of the Hindu town or village. It is an exigent discipline which holds that the ordinary degrees of empathy of the friendly social scientist are superficial because they preserve a dual perspective, that of the European social science and that which an indigenous science offers.

Its consequence was to provide an ideology to oppose the metaphors of unilinear progress and Western constructions of the world, and to advance local world views. But there were limits and inversions. The reconstructions of native categories were sometimes so artful that not every native could recognize them, although the swadeshi crafted in Syracuse, Chicago and Arizona had a familiar warp and woof. Ethnosociology was typically sensitive to categories constructed by Hindus and preserved by traditional professionals. It looked with a certain disdain on categories of thought that had once (500-2000 years ago) come from elsewhere—Turkestan, Meshed, Manchester, New York—but have been domesticated in India.

The fact of the matter is that "the indigenous" in India is now quite varied. When Sanjib Baruah investigated the categories in terms of which conflicts over agrarian rights are carried on, he found that the peasants of Meerut think in terms of caste, the peasants of Bengal in terms of class. Is only that reality native which was constructed before the Communist Party of India did over the perceptions of Bengal?

The extreme avoidance of the imported, imperial categories of Western social sciences that characterizes ethnoscience highlights two perspectives. First, for many of us double vision is indispensable. We cannot see Indian realities only through the eyes of the ethnoscientist, but must see them also through the frameworks we have inherited from rationalism and empiricism, through our native constructions. Sometimes we will assert with more confidence that those constructions are true—High Yielding Varieties make plants grow better than fructification rituals—and sometimes with less confidence—is the psychoanalyst really better able to handle a spirit possession than a family journey to a temple and its healing rituals? Second, the transformed and complex India of the 1980s cannot be grasped in terms of any single set of sociological categories, if ever it could. It is a pious conventionalism of Indian school books to say that India is a composite culture. It is indeed a composite culture and the composite frameworks in terms of which it will be understood will continue to be crafted in Delhi, Bangalore, Pune, Philadelphia, Berkeley, Madison and Chicago.

DISCUSSION

Dr. Rudolph's talk was followed by a brief discussion which focused on the development of language competence and the humanities content of introductory "Indian civilization" courses in major area study centers. Dr. Rudolph pointed out that her generation did not have the opportunity to absorb language training—the "language tunnel"—in the way that her graduate students have available now. She is watching with interest Richard Lambert's current efforts to develop a national center for the promotion and testing of greater language competence for students of countries such as India. Literature is a centerpiece of all "Civilization" courses.

Some discussion of the utility of Indian movies as teaching devices suggested that meaningful analysis would require a great deal of time. It was also noted that the Peace Corps provides an excellent vehicle for correcting one's conventional vision of the Orient.

Some Views of the State of Indo-American Relations

Robert I. Crane

I trust you will bear with me for a brief reminiscence that may suggest an avuncular relationship with this conference, on this topic, in this city. In 1943, I secured an M.A. from the American University of Washington, D.C. on "The American View of India." That began my formal relationship with South Asian studies. In the same year, I served as Desk Officer on South Asia in the Division of Cultural Relations of the Department of State. By then I had formed a close academic and personal friendship with the late Dr. Horace I. Poleman, Head of the India Section of the Library of Congress. Early in 1944, Dr. Poleman and his mentor, Dr. W. Norman Brown, proposed a cultural relations project for India. We secured funding for the project via the Division of Cultural Relations. The project involved creating fourteen basic libraries of books, journals and microfilms of academic materials in the United States. The fourteen libraries were assembled and shipped as gifts to fourteen university libraries in India. That was the first academic project, funded by the U.S. State Department, for cultural and intellectual cooperation with India.

Much more recently, a young scholar completed his Ph.D. dissertation, subsequently published, on modern India under my supervision at Syracuse University. The gentleman in question, Dr. Richard Cronin, joined the Library of Congress in its Congressional Research Division and played an active role in organizing the conference we are attending today. Unfortunately, Dr. Cronin is in Pakistan at a conference and so was not able to be with us here.

These connections with the Library of Congress and with South Asian studies, stretching back longer than I care to remember, give me the avuncular feeling referred to and also the vantage point of more than forty years of active involvement in South Asian studies and in the growth of Indo-American relations. That is the vantage point upon which my comments this morning are based.

As you all know, the decade roughly between 1961 and 1971 or so, marked the high-water point in the rapid growth and diffusion of South

Asian studies in North America, both at the undergraduate level and in graduate schools across the nation. By 1972, the high school curriculum—in a number of states—had also been changed to bring some understanding of South Asia to students in public schools.

During the decade 1962-72, the American academic environment was open and receptive to the growth of South Asian studies. There was a growing national awareness of and interest in South Asia and our national interest in that region. There were, also, some significant new agencies for furthering Indo-American understanding, such as the American Institute of Indian Studies founded by W. Norman Brown and, in New York State, the Educational Resources Center with its main office in New Delhi. The Educational Resources Center was established under the leadership of Ward Morehouse through the State Education Department of New York in Albany. These and other organizations did all they could to inform Americans about India and to modify high school, college and university curricula on South Asia.

By 1961, the Ford Foundation, the Carnegie Corporation and the Rockefeller Foundation had begun to fund and support various aspects of South Asian studies in a growing number of colleges and universities. In addition, another major source of funding and support for expanded South Asian studies had materialized. Partly as a consequence of careful lobbying by committees of the Association for Asian Studies, the Congress enacted into law the National Defense Education Act and the National Defense Foreign Language Fellowship Program. Meanwhile, the Library of Congress launched the impressive PL480 book and journal acquisition program that brought a veritable cornucopia of materials on South Asia to a number of libraries in this nation. As a result of these varied inputs and initiatives, South Asian studies burgeoned. By 1971, there were more than twenty South Asian studies programs in our universities. This dramatic leap in South Asian studies programs was accompanied by an unparalleled number of NDFL fellowships for study of South Asian languages and society. All of us gathered here benefitted in scholarly and academic terms from that period of vigorous growth. Hopefully, American understanding of South Asia benefitted equally.

However, no matter how much may have been accomplished by the great expansion of national resources for study of South Asia, none of us can "rest on our laurels." Education with respect to South Asia and improvement of American understanding of that region remains a never-ending process. Each new year brings into being fresh and challenging new dimensions of our national interaction—for good or for ill—with the peoples and governments of South Asia. Those who have a genuine commitment to the study of the region and a conviction of the relevance—in the contemporary world—of knowledge of South Asia must work to improve and extend sound educational facilities and resources. This is still a matter of national need.

Meanwhile, the context in which we now function is—at least in some respects—less receptive and less conducive to our efforts and goals. Changing times and interests, as well as dwindling sources of financial and institutional support, pose new problems, while public interest turns in other directions. By 1974, important changes began to take place *vis-a-vis* South Asian studies. Foundation funding declined substantially, while Office of Education support was greatly cut. University and college administrations—responding to diminution of external support—frequently cut their own commitment to South Asian studies and the number of fellowships declined dramatically. By 1976, there were no more than six or seven properly supported centers for South Asian studies, where there had been in 1972 some twenty-three. Only a few major centers escaped the worst consequences of these trends.

The decline in external support for South Asian studies need not have been accompanied by virtual termination of internal university commitment. That is, however, largely what happened. In general, American higher education during the most recent decade has made all too little effort to sustain adequate support for research and teaching on South Asia and by now, worse luck, the Library of Congress PL480 book acquisition program for South Asia has virtually run very low on funds. Library acquisitions face something of a crisis.

In part all of this has, of course, been a response to changing public and student interest. The rapid rise of programs for computer sciences or for training in management has put burdens on university budgets. They compete vigorously with the waning interest in programs for serious study of South Asia. As a result there has been a drift into academic "marginality," on many a campus, of what is too often referred to as "Third World studies." For traditional, old-line departments and for newer, quasi-professional programs in management or media studies, the marginality of "non-Western studies" is self-evident.

It may also be noted, in the context just outlined, that faculty members—including specialists on South Asia—have to survive. If and when the decline in institutional commitment, along with dwindling enrollments, make their impact, some of the South Asianists have to "retool" and turn their hands to endeavors that seem promising as career alternatives. This tendency has been reinforced by the fact that, during the heyday of unprecedented growth in South Asian studies many people were attracted to South Asian studies because ample resources were there, because fellowships were readily available, or because a dean or provost signalled the willingness of the university to encourage the study of the region. This band-wagon effect brought some people into our midst whose interests were largely career-oriented. The search for greener pastures after 1976 presumably posed no agonizing choices for them. The real issue was, however, the not-so-subtle shift in public and student interest that undermined the pre-1972 enthusiasm. This situation has created problems for young scholars with recently acquired Ph.D.'s on South Asia. They find it very difficult to find positions in higher education in which they can use their skills and specialization creatively.

The problem we face seems now to be: how best can South Asian studies of high quality be sustained? How, in turn, can American understanding of South Asia be improved and enriched? These issues call for our best thinking and energetic, cooperative action. The challenge we face is to continue creative and sound development of resources for these important studies during a period now marked by limited support. I suspect few among us have any magic formulae in hand. However, I would like to take this opportunity to share with you a few suggestions—hopefully constructive—based upon forty years of involvement.

First, it strikes me we must do all in our power to raise the level of excellence of our teaching, research and publications dealing with the Indian Ocean region. Anything less than high quality is, in fact, a disservice. If South Asian studies are to prosper in colleges and universities on a broad basis, we must demonstrate to higher education their academic quality, their relevance and their rightful partnership in the mission of higher education.

Second, we must cooperate quite consciously, collaborating in support for broad institutional commitment in the furthering of quality studies and the diffusion of information regarding South Asia. This is vital. I fear that failure to do this will consign the study of India to increased marginality, perhaps tolerated but not appreciated.

Third, individually and collectively we must make vocal our shared conviction that high quality teaching and research about the region continue to be crucial to the overall achievement of our national educational and informational needs. We must not allow South Asian studies to become increasingly marginalized.

Fourth, we must consult together to uncover new strategies and new opportunities to demonstrate the importance and the relevance of South Asian studies during the coming decade. We cannot rest on our laurels, hoping to be appreciated. It is up to us to show the importance of our commitment to an improved understanding of the nations and peoples of South Asia. In this respect, I believe it is wise to stress the importance of the comparative approach in our teaching and research. The comparative approach makes obvious the relevance of knowledge and understanding about India to a much broader range of academic concerns. Moreover, the comparative approach helps students at all levels better to understand their own society and history by making comparisons between their own—or European—values, forms of organization, political systems, or economic practices and those of South Asia. Comparison is a valid and useful pedagogic device anywhere in the curriculum and it enhances the significance of knowledge about so different a way of life as that of India.

Fifth, it is important for us to demonstrate that ours is not, by and large, a self-serving quest. Our goals serve the broad public interest and can help our nation to avoid or minimize egregious blunders regarding the complex public issues in our relations with South Asia.

Insofar as we are able effectively to pursue the objectives just mentioned, it would seem to me we ought to be able to make the case for national recognition of the importance of our joint enterprise.

There is, of course, another side to the subject we have under discussion here. In essence, that is the issue of our impact, if any, upon public opinion and public awareness of the position and role of the Republic of India in our world. Closely related is the issue of political, economic and cultural relations between India and the United States.

It is my impression that we have a great deal to do if we are to inform or enlighten a broad public opinion regarding India today. However successful our enterprise may have been in undergraduate or graduate study circles, I fear we have had far too little impact outside the classroom or campus. We have spent a great deal of time and energy talking to each other.

The recent Festival of India programs, sponsored by the Smithsonian Institution and a few leading museums, have had a positive and beneficial effect. Elements of the public that know little or nothing about India have during the past year been exposed to and informed about the rich and varied artistic achievements of Indian artists, craftsmen and performers. Those programs have been of great value. I sincerely hope we will, in an imaginative fashion, grasp the opportunities that have been fostered by the Festival of India to continue, expand and improve public interest in and awareness of India. If we do not, we will have lost a golden opportunity.

In any event, it seems that on the whole the great majority of Americans remain as uninformed—or misinformed—about India today as they were twenty or so years ago. The academic community has not, generally speaking, accomplished very much vis-a-vis popular misconceptions of Indian society, economy, politics or religion.

An example of one of the many misconceptions prevalent in this country is the public image of India as a Soviet puppet, dancing to Moscow's tune. Hoary sterotypes regarding naked fakirs, sacred cows aimlessly wandering in major, urban areas, or droves of starving people living and dying in city streets persist.

What is needed, it seems to me, is an organized, concerted effort at public understanding of the complexities of modern India via our media, popular magazines and the non-academic platform. Such a program requires commitment, persistent effort and, most of all, a highly imaginative and resourceful effort to communicate to a broad, popular audience. Reaching people via the classroom, that is to say, is good but is simply not nearly enough. Those of us who are here, along with our colleagues who are not at this conference, should take council together to devise effective ways and means. The task will not be easy and will not attract the careerists, but it deserves to be done for a lot of valid reasons. If we are to inform a broad public about India, we have to adopt and use vigorously avenues of public communications that go outside the classroom. TV and films aimed at the public are vital—as are other modes of presentation—to the task. Moreover, we need to redouble our efforts to influence the curriculum and teaching materials about India in the lower grades of our public schools. I fear we have barely made a dent on current public school curriculae. Very few public school teachers have had any academic exposure to Indian history, society, values, political or economic systems. Courses at any level in comparative literature rarely include examples of Indian literature.

We have a great deal yet to do.

DISCUSSION

Attendees expressed concern at the pejorative image of India in many high school textbooks, especially as compared with the more hospitable view taken of China, for reasons that are unclear. South Asia studies have low and often marginal status in many college and university curricula as well. By contrast, the emergence of Japan has made Americans nervous, prompting thought, emulation and interest. Dr. Crane reemphasized that history shows that only a concerted effort by a dedicated group of people can correct this situation and that we must elevate the quality of our teaching, research and diffusion of knowledge. Dr. Rudolph thought an effective lobby was needed, such as the Africanists have developed. Hope was expressed that the Nascent Lambert Center can become an NSF-style national foundation for promoting area studies, and that the Festival of India might provide added impetus.

Difficulties of gaining access to India for research purposes have had a serious negative impact. Professor Stanley Kochanek of Penn State has been deeply troubled by the effect long delays and refusals have had on budding student careers as well as on American interest in India. Visa problems have tended to dampen student interest in recent years. And this is entirely due to frustrations imposed by the Government of India.

Approaches to Indian Studies, Recruitment and Access

Joseph W. Elder

I would like to discuss four aspects of American scholarly interest in South Asia during the past quarter century. One of these aspects expands upon Susanne Rudolph's very interesting talk. The other three aspects relate in one way or another to some of my own efforts to understand contemporary India. One of these efforts involves developing documentary films for studying contemporary India. A second effort involves recruiting future generations of Indian scholars. A third effort deals with American scholars' research access to India.

To begin with Susanne's very interesting talk, I would like to endorse and underscore her thesis that during the past 25 years we have been watching cross-disciplinary revolts against formalism in the field of Indian studies. I shall try to place this revolt into a larger context. I shall also try to illustrate this revolt by looking at a couple of disciplines that Susanne didn't have time to touch on.

I think there may be something "built into" American academia that constantly involves a revolt against formalism, with formalism being whatever our teachers and their generation taught us, and the revolt being whatever we and our generation of schoolmates are involved with. This generational revolution may have something to do with the fact that America is a land of perpetual adolescent rebellion. It may have something to do with the way in which Thomas Kuhn's book, *The Structure of Scientific Revolutions*, fired up many of us in American academia to become the next Copernicuses and Newtons. It may also have to do with the fact that America is a country of planned obsolescence, of the "new, improved" product, of the latest fashion. We are in a land under a kind of compulsion to come up with something fresh and new, to avoid at all costs being "old fashioned" or "out-of-date."

To return to Susanne Rudolph's thesis, I grant that such concepts as development, entrepreneurship, modernization and traditionalism, with which our professors impressed us when we were graduate students, now sound like something from ancient history. But I think that's the nature of

American academia. And I trust that, twenty-five years from now, scholars will be chuckling over the concepts and models we define today as being on the cutting edge of dissertation topics and grant proposals.

I would also like to extend Susanne's thesis to two disciplines she did not mention: the study of religion and the study of theater performance.

A generation ago, the questions being asked about religion in India were being framed largely by comparative theologians and comparative religionists. Today, the questions are being framed largely by Sanskritists, linguists, anthropologists and folklorists, such as Louis Dumont, McKim Marriott and Wendy O'Flaherty.

Thanks to a great deal of work that has been done during the last twenty-five years, we now have data our predecessors didn't have on such topics as non-Brahman priests and their clienteles. We have information on religious observances of the lower castes, their deities and their pilgrimage sites. We are aware of women's religions, women's devotional songs, women's epics and women's religious literature. We have videotapes and audiotapes of otherwise disappearing vernacular, non-Brahmanic epics with heroes and heroines from humbler castes and with values different from standard Brahmanical values. These data have brought to the scrutiny of contemporary South Asian scholars entire dimensions of Indian religions that the classical scholars with their knowledge of Sanskrit and the shastras never were aware of.

These data reflect enormous amounts of regional variation in India. What is called Hinduism in Kerala is very different from what is called Hinduism in the heart of Uttar Pradesh or what is called Hinduism in the major temple-complex sites of Tamil Nadu. These data also indicate how expandable the boundary of something like religious studies may need to be. For example, in many parts of India religion is directly involved in such arenas as illness and health, fertility and longevity, mental illness and emotional equanimity. To what extent should studies of religion in the West also include these arenas? To what extent does our definition of religion in the West exclude materials the inclusion of which would enrich our understanding of our own society? To some extent, the kinds of questions being asked and the kinds of data being gathered today by students of religion in India are almost generically different from the questions asked and the data gathered twenty-five years ago.

In a similar way, scholars studying theater performances in India today are asking quite different questions and gathering quite different data from those studying theater performances in India twenty-five years ago. A quarter of a century ago, scholars were trying to identify and reconstruct classical Sanskrit drama. Contemporary performances were seen to be, at best, somewhat inaccurate representations of more accurate performances of yesteryear. Twenty-five years ago, no one was doing the kind of study that Richard Schechner has done of the annual Ram Lila performances at Ramnagar, across the Ganges from Banaras. No one was studying how young boy actors were selected and trained, how spectators became participants in crowd sequences, how actors became gods and audiences became worshippers in each night's final tableaux. No one drew parallels between the reenactment of the *Ramayana* at Ramnagar and the reenactment of the passion story at Oberammergau. With this generation's questions about theater performances, it has been possible to link theater in India with theater performances in other parts of the world, and to bring methodologies and questions from anthropology, religion, folklore and comparative literature to bear upon the subject of theater performances.

My main point in presenting illustrative materials from the study of religion and the study of theater performance in India is to lend support to Susanne Rudolph's thesis that during the past twenty-five years we have been watching cross-disciplinary revolts in the field of Indian studies. The only thing I would like to add to Susanne's analysis is the observation that in our "youthful" eagerness to overthrow the formalism of our older professors, I think we have turned up some actually exciting stuff.

Let me now describe three efforts during the past twenty-five years to contribute to (1) developing documentary films, (2) recruiting future generations of India scholars, and (3) dealing with American scholars' research access to India.

1. *Developing Documentary Films*

About twenty years ago I was with a group of scholars who were reviewing films that were available on South Asia. We arrived at the conclusion that there was an appalling lack of quality films available in the United States dealing with contemporary South Asia. The usual question, "Why doesn't somebody do something about that?" generated a trap into which I fell and from which I have not yet been able to extricate myself. The nearly twenty documentary films that I have helped coordinate have been produced under the generic label, the "Contemporary Civilizations of South Asia Film Series."

When we started this series, we hoped to enable teachers in United States schools to give their classes a "feel" for what it's like to be inside India. The model we hoped to imitate was that of the film-maker Fred

Wiseman. If you've chanced to see a Wiseman film on a mental hospital, or a high school, or a police force, or a meat-packing plant, you know that he uses no narrative whatever. From beginning to end, the audience simply watches what goes on and hears what participants say to each other in natural conversations. Seeing a Wiseman film about a location is the closest one can come to being in that location oneself.

We have not been able to reproduce Wiseman's format in our films on India. There is too much an American audience needs to know about an Indian context to be able, without the help of explanations or narrative, to make much sense of what Indians say in natural conversations with each other. In our films we often have on-camera interviews with Indian respondents. We also use narration. We constantly struggle between our desire to reduce narration to a minimum and our desire to make our films reasonably understandable to people who may have no clue who is Lord Ram, or what is meant by reincarnation, or why north Indian village women cover their faces in the presence of older men.

One of our efforts to solve the problems of context has been to publish written guides that go with these films. These film guides enable us to provide much of the background information we are unable to compress into a typical forty-minute documentary film. Although the film guides may ease our academic consciousnesses and allow us to transmit quantities of relevant information, their major drawback is that they are awkward to distribute. When a film is shown in class, the most frequent question often is, "Does anybody have an extension cord?" The important question, "Will everybody read forty or fifty pages of notes and background before (or after) they see this film in order to put this film into context?" is rarely asked.

One film enables students to see the migration of India's rural workers into the city seeking employment through the person of one man, Sripal, his factory friends and his village family. Matters pertaining to Muslims living in India are illustrated by Kasim Sahib and his family and enterprises in Lucknow. Students can understand some of the dilemmas of renouncing the world and entering the fourth, idealized stage of Hindu life by observing a film about Seturam, who has just retired as editor of the *Deccan Herald* and is debating whether or not to enter the sannyasin stage.

The arrival of the videotape age may open new possibilities for introducing American audiences to visual materials from India. Recently some students and I were looking at some videotapes that a colleague had made of a hero cult ritual in rural Andhra Pradesh. There was enough material in that thirty-minute visual depiction of the hero cult to keep the entire room of students and faculty buzzing with questions for about three hours. Nothing my colleague could have presented in writing could have aroused the same level of interchange as did his videotape. Nothing else could have stimulated so many questions or have forced him to think about his materials from so many different perspectives.

2. *Recruiting Future Generations of India Scholars*

The first generation of post-World War II American scholars specializing on India came from a variety of sources—World War II experiences in India, missionary backgrounds, and travellers attracted by the newness and idealism of independent India. The Ford Foundation foreign area training fellowships funded India scholars into the 1960s, followed by the NDEA fellowships. And by the late 1960s, India Peace Corps alumni were beginning to enroll in graduate programs. None of these programs addressed the problem of attracting undergraduates into Indian studies. Yet, if the training of Indian studies graduate students were ever to equal in quality the training of, say, graduate students in French, German or Spanish, it was crucial they begin their language and area training as undergraduates.

In the early 1960s at least two programs provided opportunities for young Americans to travel to India: the Experiment in International Living, and various church programs, such as the Lyle Fellowship program. But none of the programs focused at that time on systematic language training. In the later 1960s several colleges and college consortia were organizing undergraduate study abroad programs in India: Carleton College, the Central Pennsylvania Consortium, the Great Lakes College Association and the Associated Colleges of the Midwest. The availability of PL480 funds helped hold down the program costs for student participants. Through these programs American undergraduates could study such Indian languages as Hindi, Gujarati, Marathi, Tamil and Kannada.

The program I know best is the one I've been coordinating for about twenty-five years in the University of Wisconsin, the College Year in India program. This is a national program in which students from any college or university in the U.S. can enroll. Over the last twenty-five years something like 500 students have spent a summer of intensive language study in the United States followed by an academic year in India earning credit toward their B.A.'s in their home colleges or universities in the United States.

The languages we have focused on have been Hindi-Urdu, Tamil and Telugu, with our current campuses of affiliation located in Banaras,

Madurai and Visakhapatnam. The model seems to work. There is no reason (except available human effort) why the program couldn't be expanded to include, say, Bengali, Gujarati or Malayalam and have campuses in additional parts of India.

The alumni of the program, those who have spent a summer of intensive language training in the United States followed by course work and additional language training and practice during their year in India, occupy a variety of interesting positions today. Diana Eck, who teaches Sanskrit and Hinduism at Harvard, first went to India with our program. Susan Wadley, who teaches anthropology at Syracuse, first went to India with our program. Richard Weintraub, the current *Washington Post* correspondent in Delhi, first went to India with our program. Working here in the Library of Congress are three alumni of our program: Dan Melnick, Bruce Tapper and Ray Ahearn. So undergraduate study-abroad programs in India do seem to be a viable means of recruiting future generations of India scholars.

A new set of recruits for future generations of India scholars appears to be coming up the line. These are children of Indian citizens now living in the United States. For each of the last eight or ten years, two or three—and sometimes as many as five—second-generation or third-generation children of Indians have gone to India with Wisconsin's Year-in-India program. In many instances such students have had a head start with their language training. The fact that when they are in India they look Indian has enabled some of them to do very interesting fieldwork projects.

3. *Dealing with American Scholars' Research Access to India*

At the moment, there are probably two or three times as many American scholars doing research in India as there were, say, ten or fifteen years ago. Here, I think, we all owe a tribute of thanks to Ed Dimock. I think the way in which Ed has been able to gain support for and increase the number of fellowships for American scholars provided by the American Institute of Indian Studies is simply awesome. At the same time there is a widespread feeling among American scholars of India that it is more difficult to get research clearance to study in India today than it was in the past.

In the last two years in my new capacity as President of the American Institute of Indian Studies, I have had a chance to review on a case-by-case basis every instance in which an American scholar's research clearance has been turned down. The picture is more complicated than I had imagined.

The first thing that startled me was that not many American scholars' research clearances have actually been turned down. We're speaking of something like fifteen rejections out of between 150 and 180 applications. And quite a few of these rejections were subsequently appealed and eventually approved.

It's difficult to find the reasons for the rejections. The Government of India has said—and I think it's entitled to say this—that it is not obliged to give reasons for rejections. So when a scholar's research clearance is turned down, one is left to guess at the reason. The Government of India has listed research topics it considers sensitive, for example, communal conflicts, anything taking place in tribal or defense regions, etc. Yet, even though such information is available, some research topics that appear sensitive have been approved and other research topics that, on the surface, appear not to be sensitive have been turned down. For example, I was puzzled at one rejection that occurred recently. The scholar wanted to study the impact of film music on folk music in the area. I didn't have any idea why something like that would be turned down. It was then pointed out to me that the area of proposed study was a tribal region, and tribal regions are, we know, sensitive. In almost every instance when we have examined a rejected proposal, we have been able to identify what, from the Government of India's point of view, might seem to be a reasonable basis for rejection.

Proposed rejections are not the only problematic aspect of American scholars' research access to India. Troublesome to a larger number of American scholars is the matter of lengthy delays in the processing of research applications. Currently it is not uncommon for an American scholar to wait until thirteen, fifteen or even more months to hear anything from the Government of India. Such delays may lead the scholar to reduce or even abandon the project because the sabbatical will not wait, the job offer must be accepted or be lost, or changed family circumstances have foreclosed travel.

What, if anything, can the American Institute of Indian Studies do about the problems of American scholars' research access to India? First, I think we should, as far as possible, obtain the clearest definitions we can of what American research projects are unacceptable from the Government of India's point of view. And we are obliged to publicize this information to the American scholarly community. Second, now that computers are readily available, I think the Institute should establish a research application tracking system so that we have accurate data on exactly how long it is taking for research applications to be processed and where the major delays are occurring. Third, I think we should continue to inform the Government of India about the length of time it is taking American scholars to receive their research clearances and of the variety of "costs" that such delays can generate. Academic "costs" include the abridgement or cancellation of quality projects. More diffuse "costs" can include a decline of interest in and knowledge about India—a decline from which neither India nor the United States will benefit. If India could streamline its project-clearance procedures, both India and the United States would stand to benefit.

DISCUSSION

In answer to the criticism leveled at Indian project review and approval procedures, Ambassador P.K. Kaul expressed his government's desire for more academic emphasis on modern aspects of contemporary India. He said research on India's ancient history was understandable but wondered why there has been so much concern with peripheral tribal societies instead of with India's accomplishments in science, technology and industrialization. Stephen Cohn emphasized consideration of reciprocity and equality. There are no restrictions on what Indian scholars can study here. He asked whether Americans were being treated the same as other foreign scholars in India. Others noted that the relatively small number of American macro-economists and urban sociologists trained in Indian studies is one reason why Americans are much better represented in the rural and cultural sectors. Local Indian objections to the circulation in Chicago of posters picturing village women in traditional costumes were countered by Joan Erdman's noting that India is, after all, 80 per cent rural. American academics tend to see the old and the new side-by-side in India. Dr. Stein pointed out that much of what Americans are doing contributes to broad comparative studies. Balladiers' songs cannot be collected sitting behind a computer. India has to be understood through Indian eyes; it is not a modern country by our standards. Indeed, Americans have tended to treat India exceptionally well because most of those who do research there like it.

Dr. Stein added his comment that if those at the symposium intended to constitute themselves a lobby to promote a national endowment for area studies, he would oppose it. Scholars cannot at once complain about not being adequately sourced and at the same time be disappointed that they haven't made a greater impression on their economist, political scientist, sociologist, etc. colleagues.

Having been hot-housed for twenty-five years, Indianists need to take stock of their contributions to their disciplines.

Approaches to Indo-Muslim Studies

Barbara Daly Metcalf

To carve out Indo-Muslim studies as a distinct field of study is, as is the case with all academic specialties, surely problematic. It is not that the Muslims of the subcontinent are not a significant group. They are, after all, one-quarter of the population of the subcontinent and a good one-quarter of the world's Muslims, thus constituting the largest group of Muslims in the world. They are, moreover, a population whose contributions in art, music, literature, religious thought, and political theory and experience are incontrovertible. The problem is rather that the study of Muslims often does, and should, involve consideration of contexts that include non-Muslims as well. Nonetheless, we recognize the study of Indo-Muslims as a sub-speciality, its practitioners in the tens if not the hundreds. The purpose of my comments is to call attention to the richness of this field and to the particular contributions of American scholars in recent years.

The plural nature of Indian society has stimulated particularly fruitful work on Indo-Muslims. All work in the humanities and social sciences is comparative. Implicitly or explicitly, we take some points of reference that shape any analysis we attempt. The Indian sub-continent provides a multiplicity of great historical traditions, among them the Islamic, that call out for comparisons. Both those working on Muslim and non-Muslim populations are, in particular, less likely to attribute developments to essential qualities of the tradition when they see the other population experiencing similar developments. They are also less likely to assume uniqueness and exoticism if they know more than one population. India as a field, in short, ought to put a check on the reification and the stress on otherness we now associate with what is called Orientalism.

Let me explain a bit what I mean. Those who work on Muslims in the subcontinent have an advantage over those who work on Muslims in more homogeneous areas in understanding, for example, the great trend of cultural reform in the Islamic movements of modern times. Scholars working on the Middle East have emphasized that Islam has patterns of reform that particularly suit it to the modern age. The lack of a clergy, the emphasis on a sacred book and the value placed on literacy and simplicity all reflect age-old resources particularly salient now. All this is certainly true. But how those symbols are used and why they become important can only be understood in context. Anyone working on modern developments among Muslims in India will also know work done on the Arya Samaj with its emphases that even include celebration of a sacred book. Comparisons with this Hindu movement will stimulate attention to contextual issues that might otherwise be lost. Similarly suggestive in studying modern Islam are studies of the modern Indian emphasis on *bhakti*. In the same way, no one studying the movement to political self-assertion among the subcontinent's Muslims could be satisfied by taking the presumed identity of "religion" and "politics" in Islam as an explanation for Pakistan when they have before them the recent developments among India's Sikhs. Essentialist Islamic explanations don't work.

To put this another way, there is in the Indian juxtaposition of cultures a saving grace against assumptions of particularism. So often scholars absorbed in the challenges of difficult languages and terrains burrow ever deeper or—to change to an Urdu metaphor—turn out to have no more perspective on the scope of the world than do frogs in a well. Students of the Indian traditions might assume that the materialist or substantive basis of so much they study about human development and process in karmic theories, for example, is unique. If, however, they study the Muslim tradition, known in the subcontinent as elsewhere, they would find similar theories of how people develop and how, as a result, they behave. Students of India are well situated to see that there are other points of reference than the anomalous modern West.

A further reason why study of Muslim Indians has been so interesting and, in particular, so suggestive for students of Muslims in other areas has been because Muslims have not only been situated in a plural society but have held what in the modern period comes to be defined as a minority position. Cantwell Smith early pointed to the history of Indian Muslims as rich and suggestive for Muslims generally who, he argued, in an increasingly integrated world, were finding themselves a population which, in that larger context, could be seen as a minority too.

Against this background, then, what insights, what contributions have been particularly valuable on the part of American scholars who have studied Indian Muslims? Some I have already alluded to, but let me suggest a brief list:

First, the study of ethnic (or communal) developments has been particularly important. Outstanding work by American scholars has contributed to moving this topic beyond the banalities of essentialist dichotomies that have asked the pointless question of whether a particular population is Muslim or Indian. Instead, careful research has shown how identities are contingently constructed, the way group alliances are not a given but a product of specific contextual developments. Excellent work on early conversions to Islam has emphasized the gradual nature of incorporation of groups as Muslims and the importance of political and agrarian structures in the change. So much in local ideologies and in distant reporting assumes religious identities in particular to be timeless vestiges of the past instead of—as they exist today—novelties of modern times and, in this case, above all of the colonial context. Writings on these issues in modern India should be known to those who study areas like Ireland and the Middle East.

A second theme that has been richly documented by American students has been that of Muslim reform, whether modern, traditionalist or statist. The movements themselves have had a richness here, as noted above, and have attracted considerable attention. Albert Hourani has spoken of the pivotal eighteenth century as the Indian century of Islam because of the vitality of Muslim intellectual developments of that period, and Jean Aubin, more recently, has turned the French academic terminology that subsumes India, *Islam périphérique*, on its head to see in South Asian Islam the very core of significant developments among Muslims everywhere. India's diversity, again, forces one into nuanced and contextual analyses. The facile explanations of Iranian revolutionary ardor as traced to tenets of the Shia fall flat in the subcontinent where the Shia population, whether mountain agriculturalists or aristocrats, has been relatively uninterested in any reform at all.

A third important theme has been precisely that of the multiple contexts of Indian Muslims' cultural tradition. Islam in India has found its own expression in both local and cosmopolitan contexts that have been particularly sophisticated and intrusive. The local context of Indian Islam has consisted not only of parochial folkways but also of Indian civilization with its enduring and distinctive characteristics in cosmology, social structure and aesthetic forms. Both levels have shaped Muslim religious thought and practice, from everyday ritual to philosophy, from marriage customs to meditative breathing practices, to, apparently, the Sanskrit-like epigrammatic style of the Indian Persian *sabk-i hindi*. The cosmopolitan culture, reaching beyond the subcontinent, has drifted in modern times from that carried by Persian to that carried by English, both notable for the depths of their roots in Indian populations. The cosmopolitan cultures have had their impact on high culture—think of Bedil in Persian and Salman Rushdie in English—and on politics—from the "Mirrors for Princes" to Jinnah. Both the local and the cosmopolitan strands have sometimes been accepted without question; at other times they have been analyzed with anguish in the light of normative Islam. Studies along these lines dispel the notion that these are fixed definitions of what is Islamic and what is not, and that "popular culture" has a particular (low) sociological niche: such issues of complex cultures are of current interest among scholars in many regions besides India.

For all these contributions, work on Indian Muslims has attracted relatively little attention in our centers of South Asian studies. The field has fallen a victim to two of our post-war academic biases. The first is our division of the free world into area studies. In this division, Muslims in South Asia have been neglected by those who specialize in the Middle East on the one hand and by those who specialize in the subcontinent on the other. Probably even more significant has been the second bias, that toward emphasis on the high culture heritage. This has directed those interested in Muslims toward the Arab-speaking Middle East on the assumption that those whose vernacular was Arabic must somehow be the "real" Muslims. It has directed those interested in India to those whose cultures derive from Sanskrit and the Indic classics.

The work that exists, however, has profited from trends characteristic of other South Asian fields in the United States. There has been an increased interest in culture; in the indigenous cultural, intellectual and aesthetic systems of populations; in the study of non-elite populations; in what, in short, can best be known through vernacular languages and less conventional sources. These changes are recent. In surveying the *Journal of Asian Studies* over the last decades, I found that it has only been in the last decade that any American work at all in this field was published or reviewed that used local languages. Before then both articles published and books reviewed tended to be macro-level political and economic studies. I think the first article in *JAS* on Indian Muslims that represented, if you will, an inter-disciplinary area studies approach, appeared in 1975. In recent years, however, the kinds of sources used by specialists in this field suggest the emphases and approaches that now command scholarly interest: judicial records, memoirs, oral histories whether of businessmen or of weavers, *murid* registers, *Muharram* rituals, educational records and publications, and architectural design. Both field work and library research have moved in new directions. Current international attention to Muslim political developments has, moreover, stimulated study of Muslims generally, including study of Muslims in South Asia. A particular impetus, related concretely to those developments, has been the move to South Asian studies of researchers whose access to many areas of the Middle East has been cut off. Their contributions, shaped in a different area studies tradition, should be particularly stimulating for those whose focus has been India.

While never wanting to lose the richness that I have discussed above that comes from the study of Muslims in their local environment, recently scholars have shown increasing interest in seeing Muslims in a comparative Muslim context. There is a growing awareness of the limitations of the area studies approach in recognizing the significance of a variety of transregional systems, economic, political and cultural, of which the Islamic is surely one. To varying degrees and in varying domains, the lives of Muslims are affected by the multiple bonds that tie them to their fellows elsewhere. Indian Muslims have shared with Muslims elsewhere common beliefs, institutions and networks generated by political expansion, scholarly and Sufi ties and trading empires. They have shared Arabic as a sacred language, a common body of normative classics and the unifying experience of the pilgrimage to Mecca. Like Muslim societies elsewhere, they have shared the experience of the imposition of colonial rule which at once destroyed one of the principal symbols of Muslim identity yet stimulated the self-conscious assertions of the Islamic tradition that in recent decades has taken on greater intensity and created new institutional forms. In these changes, the Muslims of the subcontinent have been centrally important. It is in the play offered between the two approaches, the regional and the transregional, that Indo-Muslim studies promises to continue as a rich field of scholarly activity.

DISCUSSION

What is being done to create a tradition of Muslim secularism in India? The speaker responded that political scientists have looked at the ramifications of ethnicity in political life: what it is about Indian democracy that has strengthened regional, linguistic and religious groups at the cost of larger identities, sometimes turning local groups into opposition parties, and how this affects state-center relations. The Shah Banu case was cited as reflective both of the tendency of secular government to make concessions to communal interests for practical political reasons and the increased strength of fundamentalism in Indian Islam. The speaker noted that the kind of communal tensions apparent in India are not significantly different from those present elsewhere in the world. To follow from

Dr. Elder, we need to move away from explaining everything in terms of belief, from studying Islam or Hinduism, Sikhism or Christianity, and to study Muslims, Hindus, Sikhs and Christians—to see how they in fact behave.

Dr. Metcalf said that excellent work has been coming out on the correlation of the spread of Islam with the moving agricultural frontier in Bengal and Punjab, the symbolism of monumental architecture, Sufism, and a history of weavers in Bengal. Recently, Gregory Kozlowski published a fascinating volume on *waqfs*, in which he used the legal status of the *waqf* to talk about broad changes in how Muslims think of the law, society and who they are.

Dr. Elder said there was a mixed record on visa applications for Muslim studies. Communal tensions are not regarded as appropriate subjects of research, but research projects can be designed so as not to contain unacceptable approaches to studies of the Muslim community.

American Scholarly Understanding of India

M.N. Srinivas

I can only view American scholarly contributions to the understanding of India in the post-Independence years from an Indian point of view, but this may not be a disadvantage since most of the other participants in the symposium will be looking at it from the American end.

The 1950s and 1960s marked a very creative period as far as the enhancing of the scholarly understanding of Indian society, culture and civilization was concerned; and in this endeavor scholars from all over the world participated, with American scholars being, of course, very prominent. What was remarkable was not only the variety of scholarly and cultural areas they were active in, but the number of people involved was far greater than that from any other country outside India. In fact, the number was so large that there have come into existence organizations of American scholars specializing in particular regions of India such as South India and West Bengal. (There may be also other similar organizations for all I know.)

It is also true, as the statement of purpose of the symposium makes clear, that the explosion of knowledge about India which occurred during the 1950s and 1960s has not reached the educated public in the U.S. or India or, for that matter, any other country. That would have made a profound difference to the educated public's understanding of Indian culture and society, and in India, might even have contributed to making the policies and programmes of those in power more realistic. If I may cite an example: The Congress government under Nehru was extremely ambitious in its land reform programme. It wanted nothing less than the eventual control of all arable land to be transferred to the actual tillers of the soil from the legal owners. In those states which were serious about implementing the land reforms programme, the holders of such concessional tenures as *zamindari* and *jagirdari* and absentee landlords hailing from the non-dominant castes lost their land to the tenants. But where the owners were from dominant castes, they were generally able to excape the efforts of the land reforms because of their wealth, and the power they wielded locally and in the state legislatures of the people. A few of them were ministers at the state level. With regard to the land ceilings law, they fought a rear-guard action in the state legislature and the cabinet and elsewhere, with the result that the land owned by each family was split up by the time the law was enacted, ensuring that very few owned land above the ceiling.

Liberal commentators have mourned the "lack of political will" on the part of state governments for the "failure" to implement land reforms, remaining totally blind to the fact that nothing less than a bloody revolution would have forced the members of the dominant castes to give up their land to tenants and landless laborers.

Our—I mean the scholarly world's—knowledge of caste, its functioning and its deviousness as well as its pervasiveness, is much better today than before, but we have not paid enough attention to studying systematically the changes taking place in it and at different levels with a view to understanding the direction in which Indian society is moving. For instance, violent conflict between landed dominant castes and landless Scheduled Castes is on the rise, though perhaps more in some parts of the country than in others, and may even increase the quantum of migration of the Scheduled Castes to urban areas. It is also part of the overall struggle for equality between different sections of the population. In a sense, each time a Scheduled Caste individual defies a member of a dominant caste, a blow is being struck for equality which the Indian Constitution seeks to promote. I mention this because there is a tendency among commentators to see such incidents in extremely narrow contexts with the result that their implications are lost sight of.

I would like to stress the importance of the study of the policy of "protective discrimination" towards what are called "the weaker sections of society." I do not have to expound on the meaning, implications and consequences of the policy of protective discrimination as it has been in operation in India to this audience. I do want to mention, however, that it is, in my opinion, the most important existing programme for the rapid improvement of the living conditions and social status of approximately a fifth of the population of the country, and in some states of the Indian union also of an additional 30 per cent to 45 per cent. The operation of the policy in the country as a whole and in the different states needs to be studied, and also comparative studies of "protective discrimination" in India and "affirmative action" in the U.S.A. undertaken.

In recent years, attempts to extend reservation to a higher percentage of people in states such as Madhya Pradesh and Gujarat have led to widespread violence and bloodshed and to the subsequent withdrawal of the extension by the concerned state governments. But attempts to extend and/or contract "reservation" will very probably occur in different states and very likely they will be marked by an occurrence of inter-group tension and violence. All this is indeed a very far cry from the idyllic accounts of inter-caste dependence and cooperation that are believed to have been characteristic of village India in the not-so-distant past. Early last year when the state of Gujarat was rocked by inter-caste violence between pro-reservationists and anti-reservationists, newspapers commented upon the tearing up of the "social fabric" that was taking place. Given the decline of the *jajmani* system at the village level owing to the operation of a variety of modern forces, and increasing intercaste rivalry and conflict in the struggle for access to scarce resources, the only ameliorative factor was the existence of personal networks which spanned ethnic, caste and religious divisions. If this also disappears as a result of violent conflict between castes, what kind of social relations will prevail in the near future between individuals from different caste and other groups? It is obviously important to study this problem.

During the post-Independence years India experienced a number of crises, but what is a matter of surprise is that it continues to exist as a single entity and as a democracy, and in states such as Karnataka plans are afoot to give greater power and resources than before to elected bodies at the district and lower levels. The question needs to be asked: How is it that democracy continues to survive, if not flourish, while it has diappeared in some neighboring countries? Can we put our finger on the institutions, customs, values and habits of thought which provide support to the continuance of democracy in India, as well as on forces that are opposed to it?

India is a country of strong traditions at various levels: regional, local, sect, caste and household. And besides, people also have a strong sense of tradition. At the same time, paradoxical as it may seem, radical changes are occurring in major institutions, and people seem to be accepting them without feeling that in the process they are losing things of great value. All this is very puzzling and needs to be investigated. Some incidental questions which arise in this connection are: Do sense of tradition and acceptance of change operate in discrete areas? How do startlingly new institutions such as dowry in south India become absorbed into the "tradition" of the upper castes and later become the "fashion" among the others?

The fact that some of the best minds working on Indian anthropology in this country are preoccupied with what may be labelled "fundamental" problems has led to the relative neglect of interest in problems in the areas of "development" and change. Apart from the fact that this attitude devalues the changes which are occurring in India today, it results in anthropology refusing to contribute to the understanding of change and development and, in the process, the discipline is impoverishing itself. Anthropology is in a unique position to study, analyze and interpret the forces operative at the micro level thanks to its established tradition of fieldwork, using the method of "participant observation." It is precisely this kind of knowledge which the planners at the macro level lack, and are of late beginning to feel the need for. This gives anthropologists a heaven-sent opportunity to contribute to development, and in the process convince planners, politicians and other sceptics of the relevance of anthropology to the development process and its understanding. Studies of the development process in India could be compared with development in other Third World countries, leading to the strengthening of the subdiscipline of developmental anthropology.

One of the problems which the Indian government and people face today is growing ethnicity which in its most extreme form expresses itself in favour of forming a sovereign and independent state, seceding from the Indian union. In less extreme cases, as with the Gurkhas of Sikkim and northern West Bengal, the demand is for more statehood. (And there are already ethnic states in north-eastern India.) Ethnicity also shows up in the sons-of-the-soil movement which has surfaced at different points of time in Maharashtra, Assam and Karnataka. It probably exists in other states also as a force beneath the surface. Finally, in the struggle for access to resources and power, cognate *jatis* are combining together to become larger entities, and competition between such caste combinations (e.g. Okkaliga and Lingayat in Karnataka, Kamma and Reddi in Andhra, Patidar and Rajput in Gujarat) are a feature of social life, at least in a few states. There is also some attempt to organize the Scheduled Castes and other poor groups on the lines of class, and such organizations are known as *dalits*. Ethnicity, then, is crucial to modern India and demands study. The comparative study of ethnicity in India and the U.S.A. should have some priority.

Hinduism has been changing since the days of Raja Rammohun Roy and the pace of change has perhaps increased sharply since Independence. Hindu monasteries now undertake a variety of welfare activities, and monastic heads travel a good deal and mix far more than before with their followers. The latter are also drawn from a much wider social range than before. A few monastic heads are prominent in giving a new, activist and egalitarian interpretation to Hinduism. Also, the secular dimension of calendrical festivals and of ritual occasions such as weddings, is increasing. Vedic sacrifices are performed with much pomp and show, new temples are founded, public lectures on a vast variety of religious topics are popular, more and more people seem to be going on pilgrimages, and so on. The new resurgence in Hinduism seems to have implications not only in religious but in other realms. They need to be studied and understood.

DISCUSSION

In response to audience comments, the speaker noted that, surprisingly, it is some of the traditional leaders who are in a number of cases catalyzing changes in caste relationships by attempting to bring Scheduled Caste members into the main stream in various ways. This is a phenomenon that invites study in order to help us understand where it is leading. It is not because of people's deep religious beliefs that they resist modernization, but there are certain restraints that come from the political system. A lot more needs to be done with the education of children. Indians should pay far more attention to their primary and religious schools. Education must influence changes in children's attitudes toward work, time, place, numbers and other basic concepts of a modern society.

Dr. Rudolph noted that we should not assume religious commitment and modernization to be incompatible. American religious fundamentalism is often highly correlated with great levels of efficiency, effectiveness, modernity and technology. One of the things that goes with social mobility, particularly among Hindus, is that you invest your money in religious ceremonies and religious communications, in temples and churches.

Dr. Srinivas cautioned that it is a mistake to think that only Brahmans are priests in Hinduism. Every caste has its priests, as do the Scheduled Castes. But it is the swamijis who are getting together and saying things like "untouchability is not in the sastras." This is a blow for modernity.

Section II

AMERICAN UNDERSTANDING OF TRADITIONAL INDIA

American Understanding of Indian Tradition: Yesterday, Today and Tomorrow

Karl H. Potter

In the "olden days"—my olden days, when the study of India was just beginning to enter the modern era—we used to think that the problems arising concerning policy centered around a tension between "area studies" and the "disciplines." I have since come to think that this was not a real source of tension, partly since in traditional studies, on which I have been asked to speak today, the distinction did not always apply. After all, a historian of ancient or medieval India naturally spends his time on South Asia to the exclusion of other parts of the world; he is an area specialist of necessity. Things are not as clear in the case of my own area, Indian philosophy, but here the problem seems to be to get academic philosophers to recognize that Indian philosophy is not just religion by another name. Language and literature types, which then meant essentially Sanskritists, are like the historians: their discipline is their area too.

More recently I have come to think that there is a tension which is not unrelated to the area/discipline contrast, but that it was hardly recognized at all in the "olden days"—for different reasons, however. The tension I speak of is the one between the importance of understanding India's tradition in its own terms and the necessity of communicating with one's intellectual peers in the community of scholars to which one belongs. In some cases, philosophy being one such, linguistics another, the very concept of intellectual rigor stems by definition from the current state of the art as practiced at present in the Western world. In such fields as these, the scholar faces a very real dilemma: should he respect the terminology, world-view and standards of the tradition he studies, or should he adopt the technical terms, methodology and critical standards which constitute the definition of the field which he wishes to be recognized in, however much this risks distorting the subject of his study by imposing foreign distinctions and assumptions upon it?

This was not a tension felt by the pioneer American scholars of South Asia. One of the earliest attempts by an American to treat Indian thought was published by Joseph Priestly in 1799, titled: *A Comparison of the*

Institutions of Moses with those of the Hindoos and the Ancient Nations. Views of Indian religions are occasionally reported during the nineteenth century, but practically always in a comparative vein as here, the comparison inevitably telling against Indian tradition. Although America was born out of reaction against imperialism, Americans did not easily extend their tolerance of others' political views to include appreciation of others' religious convictions.

In the case of language studies, there was likewise an unquestioned acceptance of the superiority of Western methods, even after it became known that India had pioneered those very methods!

The earliest American Sanskrit professor of whom I know was Isaac Nordheimer, professor of Arabic, Syriac, Persian and Ethiopic in the University of the City of New York, who in 1836 taught "Sanskrit" on Wednesdays and Fridays from 7 to 8 p.m. A successor who had greater impact was Edward Elbridge Salisbury, who held the double chair of Sanskrit and Arabic at Yale from 1841 to 1854, and brought to it training under European teachers who had already developed their own methods of language study. Salisbury was a charter member of the American Oriental Society founded in 1842, and served as its Secretary and President through many years in the mid-nineteenth century.

Salisbury did not write much, but he taught the most famous American Sanskritist of the nineteenth century, William Dwight Whitney. Whitney's *Sanskrit Grammar* (1879) remains the definitive one developed outside India, and is supplemented by his *Roots ... of the Sanskrit Language* (1885). He translated a number of Sanskrit classics, including portions of the Vedas. He was one of the "faithful collaborators" with Bohtlingk and Roth in their monumental Petersburg Sanskrit Dictionary. Modern students of Sanskrit who are made acquainted with indigenous Indian grammars soon grow to appreciate how different Whitney's approach is to classical Paninian methods.

Indian thought was also transmitted to the general public by the Transcendentalists, such as Ralph Waldo Emerson and Henry David Thoreau. They were content to let Indian wisdom as translated by others figure in their own poetic and philosophic imaginations, but their interest led subsequent Transcendentalists such as Paul Carus to consciously try to develop interest in Buddhism and Indian thought generally, and this intention is also found among the Theosophists. By the end of the nineteenth century, the intellectual climate was perhaps for the first time in American history ready to deal with India on its own terms.

The turn of the century finds Indian studies still confined to religion, philosophy and language but increasingly of interest to intellectuals of all kinds. Swami Vivekananda created a tremendous stir in religious circles by his presence at the World Parliament of Religions in Chicago in 1893, and travelled extensively during the following year founding branches of the Vedanta Society of the Ramakrishna Order. The influential Harvard philosopher Josiah Royce discovered important parallels between his thought and that of the Upanishads. Although William James found Indian thought uncongenial, other Harvard philosophers developed an interest, most notably James Haughton Woods, who visited India twice in the first decade of the twentieth century and whose translation of Patanjali's *Yogasutras* with commentaries remains one of the landmarks of American work on Indian thought. During the last half of the nineteenth and the first half of the twentieth century, a number of great names in Indological studies flourished in this country, among them Maurice Bloomfield, Franklin W. Edgerton, Charles Rockwell Lanman, Arthur W. Ryder and Henry Clark Warren are well-known.

Of all these well-known Indologists, however, none has had anything like the impact on Indian studies as W. Norman Brown, who deserves to be called the father of Indian studies in the U.S. for a number of reasons. Brown studied with Bloomfield at Hopkins and received his advanced degrees there, then studied Sanskrit at Banaras in 1922-24. He was Professor of Sanskrit at the University of Pennsylvania from 1926 until his retirement in 1966, a full 40 years of continuing service. His special research concentration first centered in Vedic philology and Indian story literature, but his influence is in part a reflection of the catholicity of interest he eventually developed: Indian art, manuscripts, archaeology, and, most importantly, the development of modern India.

Still another feature of Brown's approach is of the greatest significance for modern Indian studies. Unlike most Indologists and philosophers, who tend to be loner scholars busy with their teaching and research, shunning committee work where possible, Brown was extremely active in organizing and administering joint efforts to develop South Asian studies. In 1926, he organized a committee under the auspices of the American Oriental Society, taken over by the American Council of Learned Societies in 1930, which developed a plan for a School of Indic and Iranian Studies in India. The Committee never found funds to implement this plan, although some archaeological digs at Canhu-daro and one or two other research projects were supported. The idea of an American scholarly institution in India remained in Norman's mind, however, and was revived as the American Institute of Indian Studies in the later 1950s.

With Norman Brown the concept of area studies was applied to the South Asian area. Inspired by Brown's efforts and example, and responding to the changing world after World War II, a need began to be felt for South Asian studies in fields other than the traditional ones. Philanthropic foundations began to support the development of programs in South Asian studies at certain universities, initially the Carnegie Corporation, Rockefeller Foundation and the Ford Foundation. The fact that many young people had spent inadvertent time in South Asia during their military service resulted in some of them returning to their studies with an interest in learning more about the area; furthermore, as in Norman Brown's case, a number—though rather few—academics had assisted the U.S. Government in South Asia-related activities during the war. The first South Asian language and area program in the United States was established at the University of Pennsylvania in 1947. In due course, many other colleges and universities followed suit.

Another result of the war had a reinforcing effect at this time, and this was the passage of the Fulbright Act, which made available for fellowship and travel support funds resulting from the sale of war-surplus material left behind by U.S. forces in various parts of the world. For the first time the U.S. Government thus came to support international studies in a large way. These opportunities for study and research abroad were increased soon by the development under Ford Foundation auspices of fellowships for training in international affairs. With the establishment of National Defense Education Act Title VI Language and Area Centers at several American universities, accompanied by a Fellowship program encouraging the study of South Asian languages and traditions, the government has by now far outstripped other sources of support for all aspects of the study of the South Asian region, including studies of the cultural traditions.

Over the past several decades, an exponentially expanding number of scholars have been able to themselves spend extended periods of time in India, and in some cases it has been possible for them to come into thorough contact with representatives of traditional Indian culture. Not only scholars. Our present situation is strongly influenced by some three generations of young people who have become entranced with Indian mysticism and music, who have viewed India as oriented away from the increasingly violent goals apparent in the behavior of large Western nations and the economic frenzy exhibited by so many of their citizens. Academics tend to publicly disown this youthful element, but South Asian studies has flourished in large part because of its enthusiasm, translated into new students each year in courses on language, religion and philosophy, as well as music and the arts, and even spilling over into less traditional subjects.

These young folks, and many of their not-so-old-at-heart mentors, have come full circle from the attitudes of the pioneers of Indology in the early nineteenth century. They have turned to the study of India precisely to escape from the assumptions, methods and goals of Western society. It is not only that they are interested in the area and not the disciplines involved, they very much want to understand Indian traditions in the fashion the Indians themselves understand them. Though by no means all of this student body of Indiaphiles goes on to translate his or her love of Indian traditions into a career, enough do or wish to so as to turn the "tension" I spoke of at the outset into a very pertinent problem which has to be faced by those training for careers and those administering that training.

I shall return at the close of this talk to some concluding remarks about this problem. I come now to the present. I shall eschew any attempt to name all of those whose efforts have graced the study of Indian tradition in America during the past 20 or 30 years. To try to formulate such a list would be difficult and inevitably invidious. Rather, I want next to make some remarks characterizing the current situation in traditional studies of India in the U.S. The disciplines into which these kinds of studies are classified in the American academic situation include those of ancient and medieval Indian history, philosophy, linguistics, and the fields of comparative literature and comparative religion, not always recognized as disciplines in their own right. My remarks are offered in no particular order of importance, though overall I hope they point to some significant aspects of where we stand.

Some of these remarks echo points touched on already. Even among hard-headed disciplinarians there is a new respect for the indigenous understanding of Indian tradition which Indians have by virtue of their birth as well as their traditional training. American scholars nowadays go to India to learn from pandits, not to straighten the heathen out. This naturally implies a healthy skepticism on the part of the new generation of scholars concerning the claims made by past "greats"; this is not just a normal reaction of the young against authority, but represents a very real impression that not only are Indians in a position to function as the relevant authorities about their tradition, they are quite capable of exercising appropriate rigor in their exposition. (This is not to say, of course, that these expectations about each and every self-styled pandit are always realized; the point is one about the assumptions which lead to these expectations.)

Closely related to the foregoing points is the fact that American scholars have a growing acquaintance with Indian academics in their particular fields and those proximate to them. This is a direct consequence of the increase in opportunities to visit South Asia noted earlier. By now more than one generation of scholars has been trained in South Asian languages under NDEA and other auspices. Their members have travelled to South Asia frequently more than once even before receiving their doctorates, taking advantage of language study abroad programs, Fulbright grants, and the assistance of the American Institute of Indian Studies and the Ford Foundation, among others. In many cases, they have proceeded to further study in the field as post-doctoral fellows, and have been able to become acquainted with their peers in India and to experience first-hand the insights provided by the view from within. The new generations cannot avoid confrontation with indigenous Indian approaches to their subjects; the tension which I began by talking about cannot escape them.

The resulting mix of understanding found among the younger echelons of American academics specializing in traditional studies of India is infinitely deeper than was possible for previous generations if only for this reason. Still another feature further enriches the capacities for understanding available to scholars today and that is the explosion in research aids which we have witnessed in recent years. Most notably this stemmed from the institution of the PL480 library program, just ending, under which a team of book-buyers sought out and purchased copies of everything published in India in sufficient quantity to provide the Library of Congress and some 18 university libraries each with a copy of every monograph and a subscription to every periodical published in the land. All this for a token contribution of $2500 a year! With such riches available in one's home institution's library the students of India since the 1950s found virtually everything they wanted for their research more available in the U.S. than in India itself.

Another aspect of the same cornucopia of riches on the research aid front is the proliferation of specific projects designed to control and organize the ever-mounting hoard of materials streaming into our libraries. In recent years we have seen a dramatic increase in the number and size of the dictionaries and encyclopedias, atlases and surveys being planned and executed. Many of these are in the hands of American scholars. One thinks of Richard Gard's *Buddhist Text Information* and the companion *Hindu Text Information*, which is now being combined and expanded into *Asian Religious Studies Information*; these periodically inform their readers of who is doing what in the field, as well as summarizing what is available relating to each and every Buddhist text known to man. Joseph's Schwartzberg's monumental *Historical Atlas* is another product largely of American scholarship. My own *Encyclopedia of Indian Philosophy* makes generous use of American talent and support, though its participants span the entire globe. The work of David Pingree in the history of science, and of George Cardona in the field of grammatical studies, provide encyclopedic coverage of their respective areas of interest. Given the availability of materials in libraries nowadays, however, there is no particular reason to pick out American products; the proliferation of available research tools is worldwide. One thinks immediately of the *New Catalogus Catalogorum* from Madras, Jan Gonda's *History of Indian Literature* covering all aspects of Indian culture, the *Encyclopedia of Buddhism* from Sri Lanka, the *Critical Pali Dictionary* from Copenhagen, and this is just a small selection from a vast number of such aids.

Efforts to make unavailable materials known and little-known literature better known have been considerably enhanced by the research opportunities under the various auspices cited previously. Mention should be made, in particular, of the Translation Project of the National Endowment for the Humanities, which has funded several translations of Indian treatises. There the efforts of scholars dealing with traditional studies are explicitly catered to, and this is an important thing in its own right, since it constitutes recognition that the study of the traditions of other peoples is worthy of scholarly attention in the eyes of bodies committed to the national interest.

American scholarship has in certain cases been crucial in providing breakthroughs in the study of certain aspects of Indian traditional culture. I mentioned George Cardona's work in grammar a moment ago; certainly a most salient feature of recent work on Indian philosophy has been the recognition of the critical relation between grammatical concepts and those found in the literature of the philosophical systems, and it has been Americans who have as much as any led the way in encouraging this recognition. A parallel case has been the recognition of the widespread importance of the concepts of Navyanyaya for various aspects of Indian culture over the past few centuries; it was undoubtedly the efforts of Daniel Henry Holmes Ingalls that led to the modern spread of interest in and study of Navyanyaya outside India. Still another case can be cited, that of *bhakti* literature in the vernaculars of late medieval India; here the new mastery of Indian vernacular languages meant a sudden widening of recognition and interest in the devotionalism of sectarian Hinduism and its multifarious representations.

It is evident, however, that the recognition and acceptance of traditional studies of India within relevant disciplinary frameworks has varied widely between disciplines. A remarkable phenomenon in current activities of the American Association for Religion, for example, is the amount of time and space accorded in its meetings and publications to scholars of Buddhism and Hinduism. Comparative religion seems well accepted within the circles of religionists. The situation is quite different in philosophy; the number of professional philosophers who specialize in Indian philosophy remains tiny and their credibility as being students of philosophy at all remains to be established in the minds of far too many of their colleagues. Comparative philosophy is definitely a borderline area within philosophy, and this is putting the matter in the best possible light.

Then, too, there is unevenness in the extent to which important areas of traditional Indian studies are represented in American Indological scholarship today. The study of Islamic South Asia has lagged behind other studies since the early days, when promising beginnings were nipped in the bud by the untimely deaths of Keith Callard and Wayne Wilcox. Nobody much studies Jainism these days. There is a general dearth of specialists in ancient and medieval Indian history—there, as in the case of philosophy, expertise is often to be found among Sanskritists rather than historians by training. The history of science, so brilliantly and seminally studied in the case of China by Joseph Needham, has been generally ignored with the conspicuous exception of Pingree's work. Within Indian philosophy there is a surprising lack of persons specializing on Advaita Vedanta, widely supposed to be the dominant if not the only philosophical point of view found in India. Finally, despite the interest in the devotional literature of late medieval and early modern India, there is little being done on the vernacular literature relating to the theologies associated with, say, the Lingayats in the south or Vallabha's Suddhadvaita in the north.

Where are we likely to go from here? I don't really care to address this; being more a preacher than a prophet by nature, I prefer to consider where we should go from here. Let me make a few remarks about general assumptions I think must be made, record the need for continuation of certain types of funding and make one large-scale recommendation.

The overall aim of policy in our area, it seems to me, should be to maintain and increase a balanced American awareness and understanding of Indian culture both as it has been and as it has come to be. I assume that in order to pursue this aim we should continue to train American scholars in the languages of India and to make efforts to provide communicative links between Indians and their American counterparts. We should where feasible try to relate Indian studies to disciplinary developments. There is a need to train scholars in the gap areas of the kind I reviewed a moment ago so as to ensure the balanced understanding aimed at. It remains essential to continue to acquire the entire corpus of publications emanating from India as well as publications from elsewhere relating to Indian studies. Finally, I assume that the pattern of higher education in the United States that dictates diffusion of scholarship on a particular area throughout the land will continue. This presents particular problems and precludes centralization of personnel and resources in the fashion practiced in other countries of the world, but it represents a genuinely American habit of mind which lets friendly competition determine policy and abhors, I believe rightly, monopoly of any important area by one person or group.

The implications for funding are, I believe, obvious. Support needs to be continued at present or increased levels for language study, for study abroad, for conferences national and international on things Indian, and for library needs, an especially urgent need in the light of termination of the PL480 program. Beyond these, I believe that there are certain kinds of imaginative enterprise which might make a deal of difference eventually in maturing American Indology.

A continued source of annoyance for those of us who are oriented toward classical or medieval studies of India rather than current affairs is that government funding can hardly help but be oriented away from us and towards modern studies, where at least till now there has been a singular dearth of interest among students in studying contemporary South Asian affairs. The NDEA language fellowship program, for example, specifically precludes awarding fellowships to students of Sanskrit and other classical languages of South Asia. Those of us engaged in administering centers find ourselves being enticed and encouraged to try to woo professional schools, big business and political bodies to an interest in India, and are offered funds either with strings explicitly attached or else subtly hinted at while we are all the time perfectly aware that there are plenty of students, research concerns and purposes relating to traditional studies of India needing to be served by imaginative funding sources.

It seems to me that despite the general pattern in American education for competitive diffusion of scholarly expertise on a given area, it should still be possible to gain the advantages which would accrue from centralization of certain sorts of resources. Furthermore, I think it should be of special interest and concern to members of the American community who bring to our shores an Indian inheritance to help in a cooperative fashion to make possible increased awareness of India's traditions through enabling some of those special advantages to be grasped. I should like to urge that attention be given to the establishment of an Institute for Traditional Studies of India. Such an institute, modeled after the Princeton Institute for Advanced Studies and its counterparts elsewhere, including Shimla in India, would provide opportunity for selected American and Indian scholars to work either by themselves or in collaboration with others. The institute could provide a venue for workshops and conferences on themes deemed important or needing attention.

This institute might collect various other needed functions within itself, depending on its sponsorship and financial abilities. For example, it might constitute a natural expansion of the American Institute of Indian Studies, possibly serving as headquarters for the AIIS, providing orientation for students and faculty proceeding abroad on fellowships and providing the much needed reciprocity which would bring Indian scholars to our shores in equal quantity to our own scholars presently receiving aid. It could endeavor to arrange for a parallel institute in India, or perhaps arrange with several Indian institutions to exchange privileges and agreements. It should maintain a generous reference library on Indian traditions and might perform certain functions of centralized collecting which seem likely to be needed in the days ahead when every university library cannot collect everything on India as before. It could, if it was deemed desirable, provide a location for specialized language instruction in those languages of India not presently taught elsewhere. It should provide publication outlets for its fellows and others in the form of a journal, occasional papers or a monograph series. It might, but need not, maintain a more or less restricted instructional program, bringing selected students, perhaps the more advanced ones, to the institute for periods of work on themes deemed constructive to the purpose proposed above.

Whether conducted at such an institute or in the standard way as now at various academic centers, scholarship on Indian traditions will operate essentially in terms of individual initiative. This being the case, it may be questioned why it is of central importance that there be collaborative enterprises such as those that would be made possible by the establishment of an institute along the lines mentioned. It seems to me that the argument on this point returns us inevitably to the tension discussed at the outset.

When I began studying Indian philosophy with Daniel Ingalls many years ago in the 1950s, he assured me that the time when Indian philosophy would be recognized as part of philosophy proper was far ahead of us for the simple reason that so few texts were as yet available that it was impossible to discern the pattern of Indian thought sufficiently clearly to present it to the general reading public. Just as Greek philosophy, now widely taught as a standard element in undergraduate instruction through translations and paraphrases, had first to be made available through the efforts of specialists on ancient Greek texts, likewise, Ingalls assumed, a stage of textual rendition had to be gone through before philosophical criticism could be exerted upon it. Implicit in this way of looking at the matter is the notion that the standards of successful translation of Greek philosophical texts are non-controversial, that translation of Greek thought will straightforwardly provide the appropriate materials for philosophically sophisticated and challenging discussion.

I am not a specialist on Greek philosophy and do not know to what extent this notion is defensible there. It seems to me that in any case it won't wash when transferred to Indian philosophy. It is arguable that the work of Plato and Aristotle define philosophy; that if they aren't philosophers, nobody is. "Philosophy," after all, is a Greek word and the standards by which one criticizes philosophy stem from practice of the Socratic method, for example. But it is questionable whether such standards apply to Indian thought. In a sense there is no such thing as Indian philosophy; the extent to which there can be said to be such a commodity depends precisely on how one chooses to interpret the business which a body of textual material is concerned with. And that is not something that straightforwardly arises from any way of translating those texts. The translator of Indian materials, though he be a loner in his field, faces in its starkest form the dilemmas arising from the tension between honest reflection of indigenous meaning and the requirements of the community to which the translation is addressed.

It is in the light of these considerations that a forceful argument for more collaborative projects arises. If there is to be Indian philosophy, there must be Indians who are philosophers and philosophers who can respond to India. The former provide the text, the latter the context; the former must become the speakers and the latter the audience. This is not clearly the case at present. Bringing together pandits who command the tradition with philosophers, training both of them, the one to address the latter in terms intelligible to them, the latter to appreciate the distinctions which constitute the rigor of indigenous Indian science, this is the function that can be played by collaborative projects.

An old Indian philosopher friend, Daya Krishna, has recently told me of a project he has had a hand in in India in which pandits have been brought together with academic philosophers of Western training and been armed with earphones plugged into multiple translation devices—a kind of United Nations of philosophy. For the first time, if all went well, traditional India spoké to a philosophical audience in their own terms and yet with a chance to communicate to an audience whose language differed. I have not seen the results of these experimental conferences, but offer this as an example of an enterprising attempt to overcome the tension that I have spoken of. There have been some in our country as well. Some of us have been engaged recently in an attempt to come to grips with a unique traditional Indian notion, that of *karma*. The *karma* project is mostly finished, and though I had a central role in planning and accomplishing it, I can't honestly say I think it succeeded, if the standards of success be considered to be anything like the understanding of which I am now speaking. Similar projects, like the *karma* project supported by funds from the Joint Committee on South Asia of the Social Science Research Council and American Council of Learned Societies, include a project on the Indian concept of the person, led by McKim Marriott, the notion of *adab* in South Asian Islam, led by Barbara Metcalf and a study of Indian folklore, led by A.K. Ramanujan. All of these arose from a planned program designed to address the problem of seeing South Asian culture from the inside, so to speak. Marriott in particular has given extensive thought to the general dimensions of this problem, and has proposed the development of an Indian ethnoscience, a methodology couched in the traditional terminology of Indian languages, as constituting what is required to face the dilemma. Marriott's own considerable contribution to this end has been a remarkable series of papers and the training of a host of student practitioners devoted to exploring the requisite methodology. Predictably, it has received little attention either in India or in the U.S. outside of its coterie of enthusiasts, but that itself emphasizes the depth of the dilemma.

My discussion has moved at a high level of abstraction and may well be earning a sceptical reception as a result. I suspect many of my American colleagues who specialize in the several disciplines here under discussion will find my message odd if not bogus. "Is there really any such dilemma or tension as Potter rants about?," I hear them saying, "and even if there is, isn't it the business of others—social scientists, say—to deal with it? We have enough problems just reading the texts." My response is (1) there really is a tension; (2) refusal to recognize it suggests either a view of one's discipline as lacking in rigor or an intellectual imperialism which once recognized should appear abhorrent; (3) translation, the medium by which textualists communicate to the general reading public, poses the dilemma in the most specific terms possible and other modes of analysis, e.g. comparison, turn on translation; (4) the problem is not someone else's—the social scientist's, say—but specifically a problem for those who read texts, since the value of what they do turns directly on how they solve or fail to solve this problem.

Indeed, reading Indian texts is a special case of a pervasive task shared by all members of any community, the task of hearing and interpreting what is said to them. It is remarkable that until recently little attention was paid by scientists to the science of understanding. Now, with the burgeoning of hermeneutics, speech-act analysis, pragmatics and a variety of other approaches to the theory of communication, it will not do any more to appeal to innocence as one's license to practice textual studies, any more than it is acceptable any more to appeal to bare intuition in justifying a knowledge claim in any other area. I would hope that American humanistic scholars, led by those who study other traditions, would sooner rather than later come to appreciate this advance, and that students of Indian traditions, along with their colleagues, would face and explore the problem of understanding others with appropriate seriousness and rigor. It is here we can make a significant input and enter the community of scholars, not, as in the past, on the fringes, but as leaders in the joint pursuit of knowledge.

EDITOR'S NOTE

Since this paper was not read at the symposium, it could not be discussed.

Although many thought the PL480 program vacuumed resources from the extreme ends of India, probably no more than one-third of sub-continental imprints were ever provided to participants in any year. When the Library of Congress established offices in New Delhi and Karachi in 1962 to collect books and periodicals for 12 participating American libraries, the program was designed so that recipients could select what they wanted for permanent retention and distribute other receipts for classroom use and similar purposes. However, almost at the outset a microfilm unit was rigged up in the Library of Congress' New Delhi office and permissions obtained to copy newspapers and gazettes; each participant chose the periodicals it wanted and was given the option of receiving bound volumes of periodicals at the end of the year. By the mid-1970s, New Delhi had restaffed to enable knowledgable screening of new titles for scholarly value; shortly thereafter participant subject profiles were introduced. In 1980, microfiche cameras began to be used to preserve deteriorating texts and government publications. By 1986, the number of participants had risen to 32, accepting a range from one or two to all languages and subject categories.

Meanwhile, a large portion of the rupees credited to the U.S. as payment for loans of wheat in the 1950s and 1960s was restored to the Government of India in a 1972 Indo-U.S. bi-lateral agreement, with the added proviso that interest would no longer accrue to the U.S. account. Since then, the prospect has become one of declining rupee availability to be compensated by increasing dollar costs to participants.

The Contribution of American Scholars to the Study of Indian Religions

Wendy Doniger O'Flaherty

My argument for the unique contribution of American scholars to the study of Indian religions will make three assertions. First, I want to show why it was that American historians of religion found the study of India essential to their task, why the history of religions, particularly but not only as it developed in Chicago, found India the *axis mundi*. Then I want to discuss the danger that has always haunted the American study of Indian religions, the danger posed by the degree to which the religions of India have been, and still are, brought to America as religions rather than as subjects for an academic curriculum, as opportunities for conversion rather than opportunities for study—and are, therefore, regarded by the American academy with a jaundiced eye. Finally, I will argue that the best American historians of religion have transcended this danger and made it their great and unique strength, have not converted, but at the same time have brought to their study of Indian religions a passion that, on the one hand, the Europeans did not share and that, on the other hand, Indian scholars hesitated to show—or, indeed, to have—because it was their religion.

To begin with the first point. Historians of religions have searched for *homo religiosus*, the Ur-worshipper, with somewhat of the same spirit that physical anthropologists have devoted to the search for *homo erectus* or Neanderthal Man, the missing link. To find the hub of the wheel from which all aspects of human religiosity have radiated, to the golden age when we all spoke the same archetypical language, before the Tower of Babel scattered us into a diaspora of manifestations. These two assumptions—that there are universals in human religious experience and that the key to them lies somehow in the most distant past—have given South Asia pride of place in the history of religions. For though India may not be the place where the skeletons of the earliest man-apes have been found, nor even the place where the fossils of the earliest forms of human culture have been found, it is, I think, the cradle of two human creations that have proved central for the history of religions: the family of Indo-European languages, and a certain pattern of mythical thought. It has therefore been assumed that, whenever it was that *homo religiosus* first came down out of the trees, as his feet touched the ground and he trod on a sharp stone he said "Ouch!" in Sanskrit and began to gather sticks to perform a Vedic sacrifice.

This belief in the primacy of Sanskrit dates, as we shall see, only from the nineteenth century. Before that, however, the ancient Jews believed that all men had once spoken a single language—a kind of proto-Babelian. Herodotus told of an experiment that was designed to determine what language people would speak naturally if no culture were imposed upon them; the Egyptians raised two children in complete silence, among goats tended by women whose tongues had been cut out; and when the children spoke their first word it was "Bekos," the Phrygian word for bread—an episode regarded as proof that the Phrygians were the oldest of all nations.[1] In our day, this line of thought persists in the anecdote about the Englishman who travelled around the world (as Herodotus had travelled around his world) and returned to England, where he declared himself happy to be speaking English once again, since English was, he said, the only language in the world in which you said the words in the order that you thought of them. No Herodotean experiments were conducted on Sanskrit, as far as I know; the evidence was deductive and linguistic rather than inductive and material. No one eavesdropped to hear if the babbling of infants was in fact a crude rendition of "Asid raja nalo nama"; yet it was thought that phylogenetically, if not necessarily ontogenetically, *homo religiosus* in his infancy was Indian.

This centrality of India in the history of religions has been both a curse and a boon, a *felix culpa*. On the one hand, it has produced a misleading impression of the universality of certain religious phenomena which are not, in fact, universal; but, on the other hand, the pivotal, liminal position of India as both Western and Eastern, both European and Asian, both familiar and strange, has provided an essential thread or bridge between centrifugal and centripetal tendencies in the history of religions; that is, India has constituted a stage on which we could see ourselves as others.

Let us begin with the first of these two factors, the curse, the role of India in spreading the gospel of Universality. And let us trace it through the development of the history of religions. At the end of the nineteenth century, Friedrich Max Mueller first began to popularize the discovery, made by some of his colleagues in the burgeoning science of comparative linguistics, that Sanskrit, the language of ancient India, was related by birth to the noble linguistic families of Greece and Rome. His work had immediate and far-reaching consequences outside the relatively narrow domain of linguistics.

At first, the Indo-European pedigree of Sanskrit provided a welcome counterbalance to the then prevalent colonial and racist bias of the study of human culture; it demonstrated that the people of India, who had been heretofore regarded as an inferior, alien race, were in fact White Men like us Greeks. The racist bias had long preceded colonialism; it had been deeply ingrained since the middle ages. As Jacques le Goff has pointed out, Europe had long regarded Indians as "the unfortunate race of wicked men with large lower lips, who ranked just above monsters in the scheme of things."[2] The medieval West had developed a myth of the Indian Ocean as a *mare closum*, "a repository of dreams, myths, and legends for the medieval mentality," a "closed world of oneiric exoticism.... The Indian ocean was a mental horizon, the exotic fantasy of the medieval west, the place where its dreams freed themselves from repression." When Marco Polo brought back from India the image of a world of unimaginable riches, he also brought an image of the fantastic, monstrous exuberance of men and animals. "A poor and limited world formed for itself an extravagant, combinatoric dream of disquieting juxtapositions and concatenations" ... India was "an Eden in which raptures and nightmares were mixed." Indeed, in a quite literal way, medieval scholars thought that Eden was located on the borders of India; the four rivers of Eden were the Tigris, the Euphrates, the Ganges and the Nile.

This view took a new twist in the Renaissance, when "the Indian dream culminated in a humanism hostile to all civilization and to all religion other than natural religion." Thus the Indian Ocean continued to function as a kind of anti-Mediterranean, a stage on which the domestication and exorcism of marvels took place—though now it was the monster of medieval civilization itself that was exorcised in India. And then, "once its wall had been pierced, the dream evaporated."

What pierced the wall was the discovery of language. In the oneiric, medieval view of India that le Goff has so well described, "India is the world of men with an incomprehensible language, men denied articulate and intelligent speech, and even the possibility of utterance; this is the meaning of the 'mouthless' Indians, which some have foolishly sought to identify with one or another Himalayan tribe." This, too, is a very old Western habit; barbarians are, as the Greeks pointed out long ago, people who can't speak Greek like us, but babble barbarbarbarbar instead.

So the discovery of Sanskrit turned the Indians into human beings. Indeed, even better than that, they out-Greeked the Greeks. For since old languages (like old money and old titles) were considered to have more status than young ones, Sanskrit was truly the Empress of Tongues, and the Indians were curators of a noble heritage—our heritage, only more so.

This idea was in its way surely a Good Thing, if only as a counteraction to what had preceded it, but in its turn it opened up a can of worms that has plagued the study of world religions in general, and of Indian religions in particular, ever since. In the first place, it was assumed that other forms of civilization could be treated as automatic spin-offs from language; that if Indians spoke an Indo-European language they had an Indo-European mythology (and even Indo-European blood). (This simple assumption remains the basis of Claude Levi-Strauss's structural analysis of mythology, a method which stresses mythemes—the atoms of myth—like phonemes—the atoms of words.) In the second place, equating India with Sanskrit ignored the Dravidian element (and other non-Indo-European elements) in South Asia—both in Indian languages and in Indian civilizations.

These two interlocking mistakes occasionally combined to produce unexpected and ironic results. For instance, when Hitler chose the *svastika* for his symbol of Aryan racial purity, little did he know that he had chosen an image that was certainly devised by Indians of very mixed blood indeed and may well have been devised by Indians who spoke a non-Aryan language. More basically, the hypothesis of the primeval Indo-European purity of India eventually produced a backlash: when Dravidian languages were finally recognized, the black man's burden that Max Mueller had lifted from the shoulders of the Indians in general was now simply put back on the shoulders of the Dravidians in particular (to the extent that they were in fact regarded as particular, since the term "Dravidian" was bandied about as a catch-all slur on anything non-Sanskritic). For, once the dichotomy between Indo-European and Dravidian was recognized, it spawned a philosophy that began with Max Mueller and still persists today, in the writings of Nirad Chaudhuri, for instance, namely, the belief that the pure vision of the invading Indo-Aryans was somehow defiled by miscegenation with the indigenous Dravidians, so that the people living in India now were not, in fact, white men like us Greeks but, rather, half-castes who had polluted the Indo-European treasure that had been offered to them.

These two misconceptions—that the Indo-European heritage embraced far more than merely language, and that all of India was somehow Indo-European—combined to lead the history of religions down at least one false path. The apparent discovery that a civilization that we had once considered so Other was in fact part of our own world somehow gave the impression (though it certainly did not constitute a logical proof) that the Indo-European paradigms were themselves universal. For historians of religion, India was (and still largely remains) the omphalos, the navel of the universe. Religious patterns found in India—that is, found in the so-called Great Tradition, in Sanskritic texts—were taken as paradigmatic for *homo religiosus* everywhere. Long after the *Rig Veda* had ceased to be effectively canonical for the majority of Hindus it became the *de facto* canon for Indo-Europeanists and, through them, for historians of religion: the *Rig Veda* was that long-sought Ur-text of which Homer, the Norse sagas and Wagner's operas were all merely variants. This habit was taken over by folklorists, too, who found that with *Maerchen* and epics as well as myths, all roads led not to Rome but to Hastinapura. In our own day, Stith-Thompson's index of folk motifs presents a distorted impression of universality, since so many of the themes to which he gives such abstract and scientific-sounding titles ("Lovers meet in their dreams: T.11.3.1") turn out, on closer inspection, to be attested only in collections of Indian folktales.

Onto this stage, set by the Indo-Europeanists, stepped the anthropologists. When Marcel Mauss and Henri Hubert set out to map the paradigmatic structures of the sacrificial ritual, it never seems to have occurred to them to use anything but the Vedic sacrifice as their defining example. Things that were like the Vedic ceremony were quintessentially sacrificial, nearer or more distant variations on the Vedic theme. What Max Mueller had done for myth, Marcel Mauss did for ritual; the scenario now had both words and music—Indian words and music. Anyone who attempted to track any cultural phenomenon to its lair had to take into account the footprints that had been left in the sands of India.

But then there entered at stage left another tribe of anthropologists—Malinowski and his ilk—who challenged this image of the world as a dream that was dreamt in Sanskrit and merely translated into all other dialects of myth and ritual. When the Indo-Europeanists made universalist claims ("All heroes are metaphors for the sun"; "All little boys want to kill their fathers and sleep with their mothers"; "All cosmologies involve twins or androgynes"), the anthropologists would rise up and counter, "Not in Samoa!" or "Not in the south!" (The "Not in the south!" ploy was invoked by Stephen Potter, in *Lifemanship,*[3] as a line which one could use to undercut any argument on a subject about which one was totally ignorant. It is a line which any Tamilist can use to decimate almost any generalization made by any Sanskritist—including, of course, this generalization.)

The anthropologists went on to argue somewhat along the following lines. If it could in fact be established that the patterns that Max Mueller had cut out in India did not fit the mannequins that anthropologists had collected from places where there were no Indo-Europeans, we would know that these patterns were not universal but merely Indo-European (or, indeed, merely Indian). If, however, the Indian phenomena were also recorded in recondite corners on which no Indo-European shadows had been cast, we would know that these phenomena belonged not merely to Caucasian man but to archaic man—the new candidate for *homo religiosus*. This straightforward experiment sounds easier than it is. It is not that simple to find places where no Indo-Europeans have ever been, since the Christian proselytizers spread over the globe, getting into everything like ants at a picnic, blurring with their own tracks the tracks of the "primordial" civilizations that they stalked. Serious as this was, an even more basic epistemological threat was posed by the simple and unavoidable fact that the anthropologist collecting the data was almost always an Indo-European, thus ensuring that every Eden had at least that one serpent in it. Moreover, it is not that simple to determine whether a myth told in Alaska is "the same" as the myth told in Allahabad. (The debate about Oedipus in the Trobriands is still going strong.) But the battle lines were drawn between the Malinowskians (who included in their ranks scholars like Margaret Mead) and the Muellerites (the ancestors of Buddhologists like de la Vallee Poussin)—factions whose names gave rise to the war-cry, "One man's Mead is another man's Poussin."

These troops still occasionally snipe at one another on the playing fields of academia. But the battle is now largely reduced to the tension between the anthropologist's insistence upon contextually grounded interpretations of religious phenomena (the "thick description" that Clifford Geertz called for) and the historian of religions' aspiration to over-arching paradigms that do not ignore local contexts but transcend them in order to give play to a broader, comparative—dare one say universal?—context. These are more matters of emphasis than clear-cut lines demarcating two distinct territories. For anthropologists make Faustian generalizations too, and historians [*sic*] of religion are also aware of the need to ground their paradigms in the specific contexts of history. Moreover, the works of anthropologists like E. Evans-Pritchard, Claude Levi-Strauss, Victor Turner and Mary Douglas remain basic texts for historians of religions.

India has played a central role in the rapproachement of anthropologists and historians of religions. Here we encounter the other side of the coin of South Asia in the treasury of history of religions, the boon, the *felix* part of the *culpa*; here, too, the American Indologists begin to play a major role. For the stunning interaction in India of what has been called the Great and Little Tradition, Sanskrit texts and vernacular performances, the world of the court and the world of the village, has forced anthropologists and historians of religion to listen to one another and even, sometimes, to borrow one another's tools.

India has also had a part in modifying another aspect of the universalist scenario that she herself inspired and nourished. The Freudian paradigm that at first seemed to be bolstered by the Indian data has more recently come to be challenged by it. The events that Freudians had had to reconstruct as the true message, hidden behind the medium of the myths as they occurred in Western texts, seemed to jump right out of the closet in India. The passionate musings of infants, that Freudians meditated upon to the scornful and derisory disbelief of their non-Freudian colleagues, were actually recorded in Sanskrit and Tibetan Buddhist texts composed by adults—adults who presumably remembered not only their previous lives but their experiences in limbo and *in utero*.[4] Thus, just as India had provided the screen onto which the Western medievalists could project their Edenic dreams, so too she provided the screen onto which Western psychoanalysts could project their most lurid fantasies, or, as they saw it, India embodied the uncensored Ur-text on which the psyche wrote directly, with no Western superego kibitzing and forcing it to pull its symbolic punches.

Embedded in such arguments were several assumptions that were not only unproven but were indeed mutually self-contradictory. On the one hand, the hypothesis of universality held that Indians were like us, human beings (and the hypothesis of Indo-Europeanism held that they were more particularly like us Aryan speakers), so that the structures of their myths could be meaningfully compared with our own. On the other hand, Indians were not like us insofar as they lacked our Western superego, or at any rate lacked whatever it was that made us hesitate to call a sexual spade a spade. The Indian authors of the *Kama Sutra* and architects of Khajuraho were taken to be, like the Samoans, naive children, noble savages still free from the inhibitions that plagued Victorian civil servants and Viennese housewives—inhibitions that truly constituted the white man's burden.

This part of the psychoanalytic scenario was a direct inheritance from the middle ages, as le Goff points out: "The dream [of the Indian Ocean] expanded to a vision of a world where a different kind of life was lived, where taboos were eliminated or exchanged for others. The weirdness of this world produced an impression of liberation and freedom; the strict morality imposed by the Church was contrasted with the discomforting attractiveness of a world of bizarre tastes, which practiced coprophagy and cannibalism; of bodily innocence, where man, freed of the modesty of clothing, rediscovered nudism and sexual freedom; and where, once rid of restrictive monogamy and family barriers, he could give himself over to polygamy, incest and eroticism."[5] In the nineteenth century, once the dust had settled on the discovery of the Indo-European family of languages, one needed only to fix either of two tiny epicycles to this cognitive wheel to keep it in orbit. For those who regarded India's blatant sexuality as an evil, it could be attributed to the Dravidian black sheep in the Indian family tree; for those who regarded it as an idyll, it could be attributed to the survival of Indo-European Ur-innocence.

It was Jung who took the search for universality down a new path—but a path that still led to India. For Jung—and for those who followed him, among whom I would include Heinrich Zimmer, Joseph Campbell and Mircea Eliade—India was the motherland of all archetypes. India was the place where one could find not only Indian hierophanies (or manifestations of the sacred) but our own Western hierophanies, in forms more vivid and compelling than those in which we knew them at home. Once we recognize that India is both Other and non-Other for us, it is both not surprising and not true that Indian myths are "the same" as our myths. But Jung's theory of the archetypes implied that India was simply one of a theoretically infinite number of examples of manifestations of an archetype that was simultaneously Other (because each manifestation was culturally inflected) and not Other (because all archetypes spoke the same language—presumably Sanskrit).

This aspect of the Jungian approach, particularly in the hands of historians of religion such as Mircea Eliade, did much to atone for the sins of the fathers of other forms of universalism. For a simple flick of the wrist demonstrated that it was precisely because India was both Other and non-Other that Indian religious forms deserved to be basic to the search for religious universals. To the extent that Indians thought the words in the same order that we thought them in—that is, to the extent that India was Indo-European—we could hope to empathize with as well as understand Indian religions, to share their world order as well as their word order. But to the extent that India was not Indo-European—in language, let alone in climate or history—we were challenged to confront the same radical Otherness that the anthropologists had hoped to smoke out in Samoa. India became the interface where the things that we understood from our own world shaded off into the things that we did not understand; it was the place where we were forced to confront not only the strangeness of things that we always knew we did not know, but the strangeness of things that we always thought we did know.

In recent decades, American historians of Indian religions have shied away from the well-beaten Sanskrit paths and ventured warily out into the jungles of Tamil and Telugu, of Malayalam and Marathi; establishing beachheads in Tamil Nadu, they have even begun to speculate nervously about the cognitive systems of Munda-speakers and of the relatively isolated tribes that the anthropologists have long regarded as their special reserved stock. It has become apparent that, whether or not we choose to continue chasing after the wild goose of universality, we must at least approach the question of human religiosity from the other end of the spectrum as well, from the extreme of particularity. We must begin to ascertain what is non-universal—non-Indo-European and even non-pan-Indian—in India itself.

In that way we have begun to enlarge our stereotypical idea of what Indian religion has that no one else has. The *Mahabharata* makes this claim for itself: "Whatever is here is found elsewhere, but whatever is not here is not found anywhere else."[6] Surely South Asia as a whole can make that claim too; indeed, it was the incredible richness and variety of Indian religious forms that first inspired the mistaken but useful belief that India was a microcosmic version of the world—a place where, like a holograph, the whole of human religiosity was to be found in each individual part of the whole. Only after we have taken at least a cursory inventory of that rich lode can we measure it against any typology or morphology of all the religious forms that might exist "anywhere."

American historians of religion have done much to advance the study of that particularity. At the turn of the nineteenth century, the American Oriental Society, based in Yale and the Harvard Oriental Series, at Harvard, took up the thread that Max Mueller had first spun with his Sacred Books of the East in Oxford; scholars such as E.W. Hopkins, Henry Clark Warren, Franklin Edgerton, Charles Rockwell Lanman and Arthur Ryder, to name only a few, made available full translations of basic Indian texts. Much of their work dealt with folklore: the folktales in the Brahmanas, the beast fables of the *Panchatantra*, the romance of the Ten Princes. These studies that emphasized the more secular Indian texts were part of the burgeoning new field of world folklore studies; they established India as the source of much Indo-European storytelling, thus supporting the hypothesis of a universal (or at least a unified Indo-European) culture. Some sacred texts were translated and studied, too; Edgerton's translation of the *Bhagavad Gita* remained definitive for many years and Warren's collection of Buddhist texts is still a basic sourcebook for the study of Buddhism. But literature and philosophy were, by and large, more popular subjects than religion for reasons that we will soon explore. My own teacher, Daniel H.H. Ingalls, now retired from the Wales professorship at Harvard but still editing the Harvard Oriental Series, was, I think, the last of that particular race of giants.

These were scholars of the old school, still laboring in the vineyards planted in the nineteenth century, Americans doing their Indology in the traditional European manner of solid philology. They wrote in cold blood, with respect for their subject matter but no emotional involvement in it; they did most of their work in libraries in America and Europe, though they gathered manuscripts in India and often learned their Sanskrit in India. They were followed, however, by a new and different breed of American scholars whose attitude to the study of India was significantly different, far more empathetic and *engagé* and whose work was diffused beyond the bounds of any single discipline. The two pivotal figures in this transitional period were William Norman Brown and Stella Kramrisch, both of whom have been closely associated with the University of Pennsylvania in Philadelphia.

W. Norman Brown is dead now; Stella Kramrisch, though very old, is still very much alive indeed; last year she produced in Philadelphia, where she is the curator of Indian art, the most imaginative exhibition of Indian painting I have ever seen, and only a few years ago she designed the most beautiful exhibition of Indian sculpture anyone has ever seen, the Manifestations of Shiva exhibit, also at the Philadelphia Museum. Stella Kramrisch lived in India for many years beginning in the 1920s; when she was very young and very beautiful, there were rumors that she participated in esoteric and orgiastic Tantric cults. She lived in Calcutta, where she kept a pet Hyena named Harshi, to whom she fed buckets of some strikingly inappropriate substance (I think it was lime sherbet or tapioca pudding); she lived alone high in the mountains where for months at a time she saw no one but the bearers who brought her food up the hill. She learned, in India, from Indians, an enormous amount about Indian religion, Indian philosophy, Indian art—about India. She wrote not only about Indian painting and sculpture but about Indian texts—her articles on the *Rig Veda* are astonishing—and about Indian philosophy and, most beautifully perhaps, about Indian folk art, *Unknown India* as she called it, now, largely thanks to her, not nearly so unknown. Then she came to America and gave all this to her students and her colleagues and to her adopted American people.[7]

W. Norman Brown, roughly a contemporary of Stella Kramrisch, was a more formal sort of scholar, though passionate enough in his way. He began publishing in the staid American journals in the 1920s, following in the footsteps of the great American scholars of Indian folklore and religion; his first article, "Proselyting the Asuras: A Note on Rig Veda 10.124," appeared in the *Journal of the American Oriental Society* in 1919. He went on to publish definitive articles in other disciplines of Indian studies, some of which E.W. Hopkins had staked out: articles on the Veda and religion, on fiction and folklore, on art and on philosophy. The titles of his articles on folklore are particularly wonderful: "The Wandering Skull," "Escaping One's Fate: A Hindu Paradox and its Use as a Psychic Motif in Hindu Fiction," "The Lady Tiger-Killer," "The Stickfast Motif in the Tar-Baby Story," "Change of Sex as a Hindu Story Motif." He also published translations of sacred texts such as the *Vasanta Vilasa* and the *Mahimnastava*.[8] But he stands beside Stella Kramrisch in my mind because of his love of actual, real-life India, in contrast with the mythicized land that Max Mueller's generation knew only from books and dreams, and for the respect that he shared with her for the folk traditions of India as well as for Indian high culture, for the so-called Little Traditions as well as the Great; and he is her companion, too, in the breadth as well as the depth which that love and intimacy brought to his writing and his teaching.

It was, finally, Norman Brown who was the first President of the American Institute of Indian Studies when it was established after World War II, making use of Lend-lease rupees to enable American scholars to do field work in India. This was the beginning of a new era in American Indian studies, an era in which funding by the Rockefeller Foundation also played a crucial part. The center shifted to the University of Chicago, where the American Institute of Indian Studies is now housed, and to the University of Wisconsin at Madison, which runs one of our finest programs in South Asian studies and is the home of the present President of the American Institute of Indian Studies, Joseph Elder. This was the dawn of "area studies" in its very best sense, a school of Indology that followed the interdisciplinary path blazed by Stella Kramrisch and Norman Brown. In contrast with most European specialists, American scholars of India were encouraged to study all aspects of India and to become true Indologists, not merely Indian philologists or Indian art historians; and they were encouraged to do their work in India, to become scholars of the field as well as scholars of the book.

This was an era of far closer cooperation between American scholars and Indian scholars, the beginning of an enterprise in which Americans regarded Indians not merely as objects of study but as co-workers; and it spawned a generation of historians of religion and anthropologists who took India seriously, in a new way. Milton Singer, still actively emeritus at Chicago, was Robert Redfield's colleague in the days when the Great and Little hypothesis began to open people's eyes to the importance of the non-Sanskritic parts of Indian culture; and Milton Singer was one of the central figures in the new school of anthropologists who did their fieldwork in India with a new respect for Indian ways of organizing data, rather than (as had generally been the case) plundering the data and processing it through the machinery of Western conceptual systems. He and his colleague McKim Marriott (whose *Village India* is a benchmark in the expansion of our Indian horizons) have trained a whole generation of younger scholars—and not just anthropologists, either—in this new way; many of them, oddly enough, work in Tamilnadu.

At the same time, another Chicago man, Edward Cameron Dimock, trained by Ingalls in the old way at Harvard, succeeded Ainslee Embree, who had succeeded Norman Brown, as President of the American Institute of Indian Studies. Dimock, himself an ordained Unitarian minister, struck a new note in the study of Indian religions; his studies of Bengali sacred literature were a unique blend of flawless philological scholarship of the old school and a new kind of empathy that understood a facet of Indian religion as religion, understood it from the inside, understood it as, on the one hand, particular—not merely particular to India, but particular to one part of India, at one time—and, on the other hand, universal, comparable in some ways (though not in all) to the erotic mysticism of Christianity.

This empathy is the great strength of the American school of the study of Indian religions; it is also its greatest potential pitfall. Scholars of religion in America tend to be gun-shy when it comes to admitting to any sort of personal involvement in the subject that they teach and with good reason: the battle between those who believe that religion has a place in the academic curriculum and those who believe that it does not has a long and ugly American history. The study of Indian religions has been subject to this problem from the very start. As Brian Smith has pointed out, "Nightmares have changed over the centuries, but dreams have remained remarkably consistent," and the dream of India entered America not as a scholarly subject but as a new religion. Among the American Transcendentalists who were deeply impressed by the Upanishads, Thoreau expressed his opinion that "one sentence from the Vedas was worth the state of Massachusetts," and Whitman found inspiration in the Upanishads, "not only because of their metaphysics but also because of their perceived emphasis on self-reliance and individualism."[9] The Theosophical Society, "founded in India by Westerners and soon exported to us, was premised on a new syncretistic spirituality encompassing and transcending all the world's religions. Such syncretism was rooted in and underwritten by certain individual intellectuals and religious leaders anxious to demonstrate the spiritual superiority of India in the light of both Christian missionizing and political subjugation."[10] This American, humanistic acceptance of Indian religions as religions may be viewed as a direct backlash against the European, colonial denial of the humanity of Indians at all. Vivekananda and the Theosophists planted the still rampant belief that all Indians are spiritual, that they spend all their time contemplating their navels, and so forth. It is, I think, no accident that the American Indologists of this period, the late nineteenth century, tended to concentrate on the secular, folk aspects of Indian culture rather than on the Vedantic; this emphasis set them apart from the gurus.

In the fifties and sixties of this century, the hippies gave new life to the tradition of Indian cults in California; and then came the Transcendental Meditators and the people who hand out luridly illustrated and tendentiously annotated translations of the *Bhagavata Purana* in airports. Nowadays, we have more sinister and more notorious gurus; the Rajneesh scandal inspired a brilliant two-part article in the *New Yorker* just last month. As a result, we face a backlash against a backlash, a humanistic repugnance against our own former humanism run amok. Not since the Enlightenment has it seemed so *déclassé* for an American, let alone an American academic, to take an Indian religion seriously. The resurgence of American fundamentalism, too, has added fuel to this fire. Religion is, more than ever, the academic Scarlet Woman, pilloried primarily by those who react against the reaction of the Moral Majority, but also by those who have always been, rightly, frightened by the power that religion has (like alcohol, drugs, sex and nuclear energy) to do evil as well as good. Even Eliade, the doyen of American historians of religions, the man whose formative experience of another religion took place in India, and for whom India remained the central paradigm all the days of his life, even Eliade has been pilloried as a crypto-theologian, as a man who attempted to convert demythologized Americans to a pseudo-archaic, pseudo-universalist cult which was merely another form of Indian religion under a thin Jungian veneer.

In self-defence, scholars of religion, especially American scholars of Indian religions, have made a self-conscious effort to dissociate themselves from the cults, to be more objective than the chemists, *plus royaliste que le roi*—or, in Martin E. Marty's formulation, "more secular than thou." Historians of religion maintain that the fact that their stock in trade is ideas about gods rather than ideas about electrons or phonemes should not bother anyone. The same basic rules should apply; the mental computer follows the same synapses and we merely change the software to very soft software. This is all well and good; it behooves scholars of religion even more, perhaps, than it behooves anthropologists or classicists to play by the rules of the traditional game of scholarship—to learn languages, read commentaries, examine first-hand reports, take into consideration the various biases of the many people in the chain of transmission that ends with us. The best American Indologists still fall squarely—and I mean squarely—in this conservative tradition.

But in attempting to play the game of objectivity with the Big Boys on the playing fields of the harder sciences, we often tend to play down the more subtle but equally genuine sort of empathetic objectivity that good scholars of religion can and do bring to their discipline. And leaning over backwards is not always the best posture in which to conduct a class; it is a posture in which one can easily be knocked over by any well-aimed blow from the opposition.

Moreover, to state the matter positively, it is not necessary to defend the empathetic study of Indian religions in this way. The best American scholars of Indian religions—Stella Kramrisch and Ed Dimock, and the younger generation, Diana Eck and Jack Hawley from Harvard, Alf Hiltebeitel, Arjun Appadurai, Dan Gold, Brian Smith and Peggy Egnor from Chicago, the unclassifiable David Shulman, and too many more to name here—the best American scholars of Indian religions have used their own personal religious understanding to illuminate and enrich rather than to denigrate or bracket their rigidly trained academic understanding of Indian religions. They have not converted nor tried to convert others, but they have regarded the Hindu world view not merely as an interesting exhibit but as a potential source of religious truth. Their passionate interest in India has not blinded them to India's faults nor made them Polyannas. On the contrary, their personal experience has made them view India far more realistically and critically than did the bookish dreamers of the nineteenth century; but they have loved India, warts and all.

Thus the best American historians of religion have brought to their study of Indian religions a passion that European scholars did not share; when European scholars went native, their Orientalism, a la Said, was of a more decadent, aesthetic sort; they were content to marry native Indian women (pillow dictionaries) and to wear exotic clothing. Americans were more likely to like India and Indians, in part, perhaps, because they had been spared the distorting historical experience of being colonizers; indeed, they had an important common bond with Indians: the historical knowledge of what it felt like to want to be free of British rule. On the other hand, a truly empathetic approach to Indian religions was not often proferred by serious Indian scholars because it was their religion: naturally they were afraid of being accused of being prejudiced (biased) in its favor. (This bias was brilliantly turned to advantage by a few native-born Indian scholars who managed, somehow, to run with the fox and hunt with the hounds, to bring to the study of Indian religions a combination of Western methodology—and cynicism—and an instinctive South Asian understanding that no American scholar can ever hope to match: I am thinking of A.K. Ramanujan, Gananath Obeyesekere, V. Narayana Rao, Stanley Tambiah and Val Daniel in America, and such people as Sudhir Kakar, Veena Das, Ashis Nandy and Loki Madan in India.)

But, by and large, it was left to the Americans to attempt to strike the difficult balance between academic objectivity and religious empathy in the study of Indian religions; to keep ahold of the old faith in the universality of the family of man while grasping the new respect for the particularity not only of India in general but of particular times and places in India; to hang on to the democratic ideal of a universal justice while maintaining enough cultural relativity to accept the possibility that there might be something good about the caste system.

There are many obstacles that threaten to obscure this ideal. In this *Kali Yuga* of professionalism, in which a young scholar is far more likely to get a job in a particular discipline than as part of an area studies program, it is daunting to aspire to the over-arching, inter-disciplinary sweep of the scholars of the old school; it takes seven Homeric scholars nowadays to lift the verse that one scholar could lift *in illo tempore*, and Harvard was hard-pressed to fill the space left by Dan Ingalls, who was, as all his students knew, a kind of Indological one-man-band. Professional pressures tend to dilute a young Indologist's Indo-centrism (if I may use such a term in a positive sense): an Indian art historian has to be able to talk art history with all the other art historians (to talk about Giotto and *chiaroscuro* and to talk about Ernst Gombrich and Picasso). To make way for this disciplinary expertise, interdisciplinary richness may be sacrificed: the Indian art historian is not necessarily expected to know Sanskrit literature (as Stella Kramrisch does), nor an Indian anthropologist to know the medical texts of Sushruta and Caraka, or the laws of Manu (as McKim Marriott does). But the ideal has been very deeply branded upon those of us who have been fortunate enough to know Stella Kramrisch and Dan Ingalls and Norman Brown and A.K. Ramanujan and David Shulman, and if we are any good at all, we will brand our students with it in the American *parampara*. It is an ideal not easy to realize but impossible to forget.

DISCUSSION

Why are American scholars so empathetic toward India? The speaker noted that not all are, and scholarship can derive from a loathing. But people who spend a lifetime working in fields they despise are to be pitied. In general, Americans and Indians tend to like each other, Indians have not had a colonial experience of Americans and Hinduism has long been treated with genial tolerance in the U.S. On the other hand, although Hindu myths and stories have travelled well, like certain wines, Hinduism has not travelled well as a proselytizing religion. It is a system of practices rather than a belief system, making it much harder to adopt than Christianity or Islam. Nor have American religious forms proved attractive to Hindus.

There is a danger in a passionate attachment, and the danger is precisely the loss of objectivity. But a passionate interest and a passionate love of a country does not imply that you do not know what is wrong with it. You can care for it and want to be there and still be saddened and angry about its tragedies and mistakes.

Translations from Indian literatures have been coming in greater numbers—some fine ones in Tamil, Bengali and Hindi. But for political reasons, NEH is currently less interested in underwriting translations of Indian literary works than it is in gaining access to the literatures of China and the Islamic countries.

NOTES

1. Herodotus, *History*, 2.2.
2. Jacques le Goff, "The Medieval West and the Indian Ocean: an Oneiric Horizon," pp. 189-200 of *Time, Work and Culture in the Middle Ages*, transl. by Arthur Goldhammer (University of Chicago Press, 1980).
3. Stephen Potter, *Lifemanship, or The Art of Getting Away With It Without Being an Absolute Plonk* (New York, 1950), pp. 26-8.
4. Wendy O'Flaherty, *Women, Androgynes and Other Mythical Beasts* (University of Chicago, 1980), pp.107-8.
5. Jacques le Goff, op. cit., pp.189-200.
6. *Mahabharata* (Critical edition), 1.1.23 and 1.56.34.

7. Heinrich Zimmer, another great scholar with a personal empathy for Hinduism, was, like Stella Kramrisch, German-born and left Europe to make his great scholarly contribution in America. For details of the life of Stella Kramrisch, see the biographical essay in *Exploring India's Sacred Art*, selected writings of Stella Kramrisch, edited, with a biographical essay, by Barbara Stoler Miller (University of Pennsylvania Press, 1983).
8. For a full bibliography of the writings of W. Norman Brown, see *India and Indology: Selected Articles by W. Norman Brown*, edited by Rosane Rocher (Delhi, Motilal Banarsidass, 1978).
9. Brian K. Smith, "Western Views of Eastern Religions," *New World Outlook*, United Methodist Church, 1986.
10. Ibid.

South Asian Studies in 1986

George L. Hart

We are all familiar with the sudden growth that South Asian studies took in the late 1960s. New programs were set up in many universities, libraries began to get materials in modern languages and many students were produced. These programs have been in place for about twenty years now, with continual support from the U.S. Government.

It is not a simple matter to judge the success of South Asian studies in this period. Perhaps the greatest accomplishment has been the creation of a number of departments of South Asian studies, and the acceptance of the field (or area) in a more general way than before. Yet, twenty years is not much time, and many of the problems in South Asian studies that one could discern twenty years ago still exist.

Chief among these is the perhaps inevitable fact that the field is fragmented. Of course, South Asian studies includes virtually all of the disciplines of the humanities and social sciences; it is not particularly surprising that an economist does not have much to say to a classicist even though both happen to study South Asia. But there is a more fundamental and damaging fragmentation that I have observed: between those who have a classical orientation and those who have a modern orientation.

This has a historical explanation: when the new programs were set up in the late 1960s, the only area of South Asian studies that had an accepted position in universities was Sanskrit, which has been taught in this country for more than a century. That language was seen as the only really important cultural tongue of South Asia, having an enormous literature and being closely allied with Greek and Latin. There were a significant number of Sanskritists employed in American universities who knew little of modern Indian languages, and whose awareness of India was largely confined to the relatively narrow outlook and literature of Sanskrit and, perhaps, Prakrit and Pali.

When the new programs in South Asian studies were started, those instrumental in setting them up and determining their shape realized that modern language instruction would have to be a central part of the new curricula. Unfortunately, there were few Sanskritists who were qualified to teach modern languages, and so the new modern languages were taught by students of linguistics. This, of course, was not bad in itself; indeed, it was quite good to begin with a linguistic perspective on the living South Asian languages. But it had the unfortunate effect of cutting off the Sanskritists from the new programs, as they often did not feel they had much in common with the new linguists.

Over the years, the Sanskritists, given a firm notion of their identity by the long continuity of the discipline, have tended to be conservative, accepting traditional ways of understanding South Asia and advancing few new and innovative ideas. Those who deal with modern India, on the other hand, have had to deal with a very different situation: an enormous and incredibly varied culture for whose understanding we have few successful models. The result has been excess in both directions. The classicists have often seen India in purely classical terms, supposing that Manu actually does explain Indian society, or that the Vedas are the major source of Hinduism. The modernists, on the other hand, have produced many theories, some of which are quite brilliant, but none of which seems quite satisfactory.

Both of these groups have produced literatures, huge collections of ideas and opinions that have acquired momentum and taken on the air of inarguable truth. Each new generation of students reads the classical secondary works in, say, South Asian anthropology or history and accepts what they say—at least to some extent. Yet the ideas contained in these works are often just speculation, and sometimes are wrong. When I taught South Asian civilization a short time ago, I encountered such an example vividly: every general introductory book I could find said that the Aryan invaders encountered a dark, flat-nosed aboriginal population in South Asia whom they despised. Yet the only reference in Vedic literature I have ever located to such "flat-nosed" aborigines is generally interpreted to mean "mouthless" (*an-ās*) rather than nose-less (*a-nās*) (*Ṛg Veda* 5.29.10), as the verse obviously refers to the fact that they cannot speak properly. Such examples could be multiplied in profusion.

Nor have there been any notable and exciting general theories proposed over the last ten years. Almost everyone agrees that the older ideas—such as Sanskritization or "Big *versus* Little Tradition—have been extremely useful, but that they have major problems and can no longer be accepted as they were proposed. Yet we see no new theories to replace them.

It seems to me, then, that the field of South Asian studies is stuck in a period in which new and exciting ideas are rare or non-existent. Some have tried to put a favorable light on this situation by saying that we are in a period of assimilation, analyzing the old theories in light of new data to determine how much validity there is in them and to develop new ideas. There is some truth in this: our access to many areas of South Asian studies (such as folk literature) has increased enormously in the last ten or fifteen years. And we now have at least a few good translations of works that were not written in Sanskrit (as well as reliable translations of basic Sanskrit works that were not available before). But this process is only beginning and has not yet spawned any new perspectives or theories that are especially notable.

What must happen now to revitalize the field of South Asian studies is a multifaceted process. First, we must abandon our obsession with Sanskrit and classical studies and place them in their proper perspective. It is not much use to the field if Sanskrit scholars write dry articles on infinitesimal points of grammar or interpretation; rather, we need new and vital access to the Sanskrit tradition—new translations to replace the old, Victorian ones (these have begun to appear); new histories of the literature (these have not); new overall perspectives. Above all, we need Sanskritists who are learned in other areas of South Asian and Western culture, who can write from a wide perspective.

Second, we must increase the number of scholars who know modern South Asian languages. I do not know the exact figures, but I suspect that Sanskrit is still taught more widely in the United States than all other Indian languages combined. Harvard still has a department of Sanskrit and Indian Studies. The only modern languages regularly taught in more than one place to my knowledge are Hindi-Urdu and Tamil. The list of languages not taught at all in the United States (at least on a regular basis) is long—Kannada, Malayalam, Marathi, Oriya, Assamese, Sinhalese. This must change. We must produce more scholars versed in current Indian languages who can use them well and give us access to the enormous wealth of material in each of them. With one or two exceptions, we possess no translations from modern Indian languages that are even acceptable.

Finally, we must begin to develop new perspectives on South Asia, to generate radically new ideas. For me, the key to this process is access to the primary literatures. We should, for a time at least, ignore what has been written about India in the past and rather base ourselves on the still, small—but nevertheless significant—quantity of primary materials that have been well translated (or otherwise made available to us—the field work of anthropologists, for example). The new ideas that we are able to generate in this way will be often deficient, but they will be as valid as the ideas we have inherited. And ultimately they will lead to new revitalization of the field of South Asian studies and to an awareness on the part of others of the enormous richness and importance of the area.

For the future, there are some encouraging signs. Most important, perhaps, is the fact that more and more primary sources are becoming available to us in reliable and often readable translations. Some of the credit for this goes to the translation program of the National Endowment for the Humanities. But this, unfortunately, is not true of modern South Asian literatures, for which we desperately need readable English versions. There are also signs of a broadening of the classical side of South Asian studies: Sanskritists becoming interested in psychology, modern Indian literatures and Dravidian traditions, for example. The discovery of South Asian folk literature some years ago has helped this process, bringing together scholars interested in Sanskrit epic traditions with modernists studying living oral literatures. Another factor that will be more and more important in the future is the growing community of people from South Asia in North America. Many of these South Asians are vitally interested in their culture and literature and many interact with the academic community. They are a strong force for the strengthening of the modern component of South Asian programs, particularly in languages and literatures.

Yet we have only made a beginning. The impetus that began in the late 1960s is largely spent, and the field has become too complacent, too lacking in dynamism and excitement. Expansion, it would seem, has stopped far before the majority of American universities have a significant South Asian component. Several of the best scholars produced in the last five years have left the field because they could find no good opportunities for employment. In spite of the significant progress we have made, much more needs to be done, for South Asia (especially modern South Asia) is too important for it to languish in the relative obscurity in which it exists in most American universities.

DISCUSSION

Initial comments suggested it might be useful to have periods of theorizing followed by periods of assimilation; Dr. Rudolph thought that major early paradigms are usually replaced by the understanding that paradigms are nearly always wrong. Scholars have gained general understandings such as that Indian history needs to be approached from the village- and district-record level rather than from the Viceroy's office.

Others commented that the quality of the translations now being done by Americans, such as Barbara Stoler Miller's *Bhagavad-Gita*, are both rigorous in their attention to philology and far more readable than their predecessors, and the growing number of regional societies, such as the South India group, can be catalysts for the encouragement of translations of modern literature. Some of the major works have to be brought into the current American linguistic and literary milieu, otherwise there is no hope that a wider audience will ever look at them. This was not possible with the unattractive, often indigestible translations available in the past, including excerpts in *Sources of Indian Tradition*, although Ainslee Embree is now reportedly updating *Sources*.

Dr. Ramanujan commented that scholarship is more often a home-centered tradition in India than in any other culture he knows. His mother was widely consulted in her home because of her traditional knowledge.

The *Bhagavad-Gita*: Translating across Cultures

Barbara Stoler Miller

Soon after I completed my recent translation of the *Bhagavad-Gita* (New York, Bantam Books/Columbia University Press, 1986), a friend told me a story about a Frenchman and an Englishman who were standing on a beach pointing to the sky and arguing violently in their respective languages, one claiming he was looking at the moon, the other at the sun. As they were about to fall to blows, a third man approached and they stopped to let him translate. He looked up at the sky, shrugged his shoulders and said, "I don't know; I'm a stranger here." This is one kind of translator, who refuses to deal with the reality that translation is never merely a transfer from one language to another, but a transfer of culture.

The other kind of translator is, I think, one who struggles to find a voice in one culture for the ideas of another. When confronting a literature as complex as that of India, it is impossible to limit the unit of translation; one must pay attention to syllables, words, verses, tropes, episodes, epics, whole imaginative universes. In order to capture the meaning of a single image or concept the translator must draw in the entire culture and somehow find a way to map aspects of that culture onto the appropriate sets of relations in his own culture, thus establishing a dynamic relationship between the original and the translated version. It is a relationship in which every modification of the translation takes its own context and the context of the original into fresh account. The goal of a translator is to activate the sympathetic imagination of the English reader and enable him to confront a concrete example of another culture in its own terms.

How does one attempt to capture the imaginative universe of a text like the *Bhagavad-Gita*? There are many aspects to the process. My students and I have found Henry David Thoreau's encounter with the *Gita* particularly helpful in penetrating our own American understanding of the text. Thoreau's reading of the *Gita* intrigued me long before I decided to undertake a new translation—a decision not taken lightly because to translate the *Gita* is to confront an exemplary text of Hindu culture that contains some of its central ideas expressed in powerful dovetailing images of war and interior struggle.

The Sanskrit title *Bhagavad-Gita* has usually been interpreted to mean "Song of the Lord," but this is misleading. It is not a lyric, but a philosophical poem composed in the form of a dialogue between the warrior Arjuna and his charioteer, the god Krishna. The dramatic moral crisis that is central to the *Bhagavad-Gita* has inspired centuries of Indian philsophers and practical men of wisdom as well as Western thinkers like Thoreau, Emerson and Eliot. Interpretations of the *Gita*, as it is commonly referred to in India, are as varied as the figures who have commented on it. From Shankara, the classical Vedanta philosopher of the eighth century, to Mahatma Gandhi, the leader of India's independence struggle in the twentieth century, each thinker has emphasized the path to liberation suited to his view of reality. These interpretations reflect the intentionally multifacted message of Krishna's teaching. Its significance for modern Hindu life continues to be debated in India today.

As we listen to the *Bhagavad-Gita* today, we can understand the paralyzing conflict Arjuna suffers in realizing that his enemies are his own kinsmen and teachers. We can sympathize with his impulse to shrink from the horror of violence he sees in the human condition and we can learn from the ways Krishna teaches him to recognize his own and others' mortality. Krishna's exposition of the relationship between death, sacrifice and devotion dramatizes the idea that one must heroically confront death in order to transcend the limits of worldly existence. We may not share Arjuna's developing faith in Krishna's authority or be convinced by Krishna's insistence that one must perform one's sacred duty, even though it violates personal desires. But if we listen carefully to the compelling imagery and arguments of the discourse, we as Americans are forced to confront a far different culture than that of our everyday world.

The *Gita* has been translated into English and other Western languages in many varied forms since the first English version was published by Charles Wilkins in 1785. The reception of this text reflects broader Western responses to Indian culture. Westerners have been discovering India since antiquity, when members of Alexander the Great's expedition to India in the fourth century B.C. recorded their impressions in terms of fabulous exoticism. A tradition of myths and fables about India continued to appear in the travel accounts of Greek and Latin authors, and centuries afterwards in the writings of Arab historians and Portuguese missionaries. Not until the last half of the eighteenth century were there serious attempts to study Indian literature. Sir William Jones, a judge of the Supreme Court in Calcutta and a linguist of considerable talent, recognized the relationship of European languages to Persian and Sanskrit, rejecting the prevalent view that all languages were derived from Hebrew, which had been garbled in the Tower of Babel. With his friend Charles Wilkins, a merchant in the service of the East India Company in Bengal, Jones produced the first direct translations of Sanskrit works into English. The *Bhagavad-Gita* was followed by Wilkins' translation of the *Hitopadesa* (1787), Jones' *Sakuntala* (1789), the *Gitagovinda* (1792) and the *Institutes of Hindoo Law* (1794). As these translatons circulated in Europe and America, they formed the basis of modern Western conceptions of ancient Indian culture. Despite growing sympathy for Indian literature by the German writers Schlegel and Goethe and by Emerson and Thoreau in America, Western response was generally negative.

James Mill in *A History of British India*, published in 1817, argued that even when an Indian text might appear sensible, it inevitably contained some "monstrous exhibition," such as Krishna's theophany in the *Gita*. Thomas Babington Macaulay in his "Minute on Education," written in 1835 to justify the decision that all higher education in British India supported by government funds was to be conducted in the English language according to the curriculum prevalent in English schools, epitomized the dominant colonial attitude of the time:

> I have no knowledge of either Sanskrit or Arabic. But I have done what I could to form a correct estimate of their value. I have read translations of the most celebrated Arabic and Sanskrit works. I have conversed both here and at home with men distinguished by their proficiency in the Eastern tongues. I am quite ready to take the Oriental learning at the valuation of the Orientalists themselves. I have never found one among them who could deny that a single shelf of a good European library was worth the whole native literature of India and Arabia.

During the same period, as Milton Singer pointed out in his essay, "Passage to More Than India" (*When a Great Tradition Modernizes* (Chicago)), about three quarters of the ships docked in the port of Calcutta were American vessels. For almost half a century (since 1799), members of the Salem, Massachusetts, East India Marine Society, an association of sea captains and factors, had dedicated themselves to keeping journals of each voyage and collecting articles of curiosity. One of the important articles of trade was ice, which these merchants transported to sell in India. In the "Pond in Winter" section in *Walden*, the book named for the pond in Concord where Thoreau lived from 1845 to 1847, the poet recorded his thoughts on the ice from Walden Pond in relation to India:

> Thus it appears that the sweltering inhabitants of Charleston and New Orleans, of Madras and Bombay and Calcutta, drink at my well. In the morning I bathe my

intellect in the stupendous and cosmogonal philosophy of the Bhagavat Geeta, since whose composition years of the gods have elapsed, and in comparison with which our modern world and its literature seem puny and trivial, and I doubt if that philosophy is not to be referred to a previous state of existence, so remote in its sublimity from our conceptions. I lay down my book and go to my well for water and lo! there I meet the servant of the Brahmin, the priest of Brahma and Vishnu and Indra, who still sits in his temple on the Ganges reading the Vedas, or dwells at the root of a tree with his crust and water jug. I meet his servant come to draw water for his master, and our buckets as it were grate together in the same well. The pure Walden water is mingled with the sacred water of the Ganges.

An attempt to understand Thoreau's response to the *Gita* is to gain an American perspective on the central issues of Krishna's discourse. In this process, the text itself becomes a way of reflecting on what is close at hand.

Among the many works of Asian literature that were studied in Concord, Massachusetts in the mid-nineteenth century, few were more influential than the *Bhagavad-Gita*. Emerson wrote of it in his journal of 1845:

I owed ... a magnificent day to the Bhagavat Geeta. It was the first of books; it was as if an empire spoke to us, nothing small or unworthy, but large, serene, consistent, the voice of an old intelligence which in another age and climate had pondered and thus disposed of the same questions which exercise us.

References to the *Gita* are found throughout Emerson's journals and letters, where he frequently quotes from the 1785 translation of Charles Wilkins, on which Thoreau's readings are also based. Emerson is chiefly interested in Krishna's teaching that works must be done without thought of reward and that a person may have a tranquil mind even in activity.

The fascination that the *Gita* held for Thoreau and Emerson is only one component of their work, but it is the component most likely to perplex students of Western thought. By attempting to penetrate the levels at which they deliberately incorporated the "exotic" concepts and images of Hindu literature into their life and work, one can gain fresh insights into their thought and the thought of the ancient Indian sages with whom they felt such strong affinities. The Asian texts Thoreau and Emerson were reading presented ideas that strengthened their critique of eighteenth century rationalism and nineteenth century materialism, while providing a new set of images, myths and concepts expressive of man's spiritual energy.

In *Walden*, Thoreau expresses his response to the *Gita* in several places, which should be read against the background of his commentary on the text in his earlier work, *A Week on the Concord and Merrimack Rivers*. In the chapter "Monday," he says:

The wisest conservatism is that of the Hindoos. "Immemorial custom is transcendent law," says Menu. That is, it was the custom of the gods before men used it. The fault of our New England custom is that it is memorial. What is morality but immemorial custom? Conscience is the chief of conservatives. "Perform the settled functions," says Kreeshna in the Bhagavat Geeta, "action is preferable to inaction. The journey of thy mortal frame may not succeed from inaction."—"A man's own calling with all its faults ought not to be forsaken. Every undertaking is involved in its faults as the fire in its smoke."—"The man who is acquainted with the whole should not drive those from their works who are slow of comprehension and less experienced than himself."—"Wherefore, O Arjoon, resolve to fight"—is the advice of the God to the irresolute soldier who fears to slay his best friends. It is a sublime conservatism: as wide as the world and as unwearied as time; preserving the universe with Asiatic anxiety in that state in which it appeared to their minds ... The end is an immense consolation, eternal absorption in Brahma.

Thoreau is clearly impressed by Krishna's critique of inaction, but he is reluctant to accept the morality of Krishna's argument, despite its being what he calls the "wisest conservatism." On one level, the *Gita* does appear to justify violence. Arjuna is urged by Krishna to go to war against his kinsmen-enemies because war is his duty as a warrior and because death is inevitable. But the *Gita* is not a justification of war, nor does it propound a war-making mystique, as men of peace like Mahatma Gandhi and the Trappist monk Thomas Merton knew when they read it. Merton argues the point with clarity in his essay, "The Significance of the *Bhagavad Gita*:"

Arjuna has an instinctive repugnance for war, and that is the chief reason why war is chosen as the example of the most repellent kind of duty. The *Gita* is saying that even in what appears to be the most "unspiritual," one can act with pure intentions and thus be guided by Krishna consciousness. This consciousness itself will impose the most strict limitations on one's use of violence because that use will not be directed by one's own selfish interests, still less by cruelty, sadism and blood lust.

Another sympathetic reader of the *Gita*, E.M. Forster, writing about it in the *Cambridge Review* in 1920, during the period he was working on *A Passage to India*, deals with the issue of action and war in similar terms. Forster points to three reasons why Arjuna must fight: the first assumes that death is negligible; the second that duty is sacred. Krishna's third reason is the most profound: it takes up the problem of renunciation and attempts to harmonize the needs of life with eternal truth. Forster interprets it this way:

The saint may renounce action but the soldier, the citizen, the practical man generally—they should renounce not action but its fruits. It is wrong for them to be idle; it is equally wrong to desire a reward for industry. It is wrong to shirk destroying civilization and one's kindred and friends, equally wrong to hope for dominion afterwards. When all such hopes and desires are dead, fear dies also and freed from all attachments the "dweller in the body" will remain calm while the body performs its daily duty and will be unstained by sin, as is the lotus leaf by the water of the tank. It will attain to the eternal peace that is offered to the practical man as well as to the devotee. It will have abjured the wages of action, which are spiritual death, and gained in their place a vision of the divine.

For Thoreau, with his interest in the interpenetration of places and states of mind, the imagery of Arjuna's heroic struggle to know himself on the spiritual battlefield of Kuru gave the *Gita* personal significance. There are clues to this in his discussion of the *Gita* and what it means to be a hero in *A Week on the Concord and Merrimack Rivers*. If one reads the parable of the artist of Kooroo in the conclusion of *Walden* from this perspective, it seems to be Thoreau's own translation of Krishna's teaching into artistic terms. The artist's skilled dedication to the perfect work is what Krishna means by spiritual discipline. It is in a state of total involvement that one finds liberation from time.

There was an artist in the city of Kooroo who was disposed to strive after perfection. One day it came into his mind to make a staff. Having considered that in an imperfect work time is an ingredient, but in a perfect work time does not enter, he said to himself, it shall be perfect in all respects, though I should do nothing else in my life. He proceeded instantly to the forest for wood, being resolved that it should not be made of unsuitable material; and as he searched for and rejected stick after stick, his friends gradually deserted him, for they grew old in their works and died, but he grew not older by a moment. His singleness of purpose and resolution and his elevated piety endowed him, without his knowledge, with perennial youth. As he made no compromise with Time, Time kept out of his way, and only sighed at a distance because he could not overcome him. Before he had found a stick in all respects suitable, the city of Kooroo was a hoary ruin, and he sat on one of its mounds to peel the stick. Before he had given it the proper shape the dynasty of the Candahars was at an end, and with the point of the stick he wrote the name of the last of the race in the sand and then resumed his work. By the time he had smoothed and polished the staff, Kalpa was no longer the pole star, and ere he had put on the ferrule and the head adorned with precious stones, Brahma had awoke and slumbered many times. But why do I stay to mention these things? When the finishing stroke was put to his work, it suddenly expanded before the eyes of the astonished artist into the fairest of all creations of Brahma. He had made a new system in making a staff, a world with full and fair proportions, in which, though the old cities and dynasties had passed away, fairer and more glorious ones had taken their places. And now, he saw by the heap of shavings still fresh at his feet, that for him and his work the former lapse of time had been an illusion, and that no more time had elapsed than is required for a single scintillation from the brain of Brahma to fall on and inflame the tinder of a mortal brain. The material was pure and his art was pure; how could the result be other than wonderful?

Thoreau was awed by his own observation that the mass of his fellow men led "lives of quiet desperation." He sought to discover freedom from that desperation by refusing to be led by the senses and passions, by living deliberately, by simplifying his life in order to internalize the solitude of a place in nature. He lived at Walden for two years and two months, during which time he confined his desires and his actions in such a way that he strove to overcome the limitations of time and absorb himself in nature.

The ascetic, mystical attitude toward nature that brought Thoreau to Walden Pond gave him access to the central teaching of the *Gita*. He perceived the discipline of living in nature as a path leading toward self-knowledge and spiritual realization. He writes in his journal in 1841:

One may discover the root of a Hindoo religion in his own private history when, in the silent intervals of the day or night, he does sometimes inflict on himself like austerities with stern satisfaction.

In *Walden* he emphatically states, "My purpose in going to Walden Pond was not to live cheaply nor to live dearly there, but to transact some private business with the fewest obstacles." Walden was for Thoreau a spiritual retreat where he strove to deepen his understanding of his existence and through this understanding to gain release from the terrible bondage of life's compelling illusions. In Indian terms, it was the retreat of a yogi who carefully practiced spiritual discipline. In a letter of 1849 to his friend, H.G.O. Blake, he wrote about yoga and its private meaning for him:

"Free in this world as the birds in the air, disengaged from every kind of chains, those who practice the yoga gather in Brahma the certain fruits of their works." Depend upon it that, rude and careless as I am, I would fain practice the yoga faithfully. "The yogi, absorbed in contemplation, contributes in his degree to creation; he breathes a divine perfume, he hears wonderful things. Divine forms traverse him without tearing him, and, united to the nature which is proper to him, he goes, he acts as animating original matter." To some extent and at rare intervals even I am a yogi.

DISCUSSION

In teaching the *Bhagavad-Gita*, Dr. Stoler Miller said she incorporates reading of T.S. Eliot, especially the *Lovesong of J. Alfred Prufrock*, and Whitman. The *Gita* is controversial and its use for the advocacy of violence needs to be explored. It should be taught as a text and not as gospel. Amid comments on the welcome appearance of such translations in the U.S., it was noted that it is not clear to what extent classics such as the *Gita* are being revived in India. There have been efforts at popularization, including use of television, and there has been an explosion of regional literature.

Contributors from the audience added that during the Emerson-Thoreau era, Americans were involved in some of the religious revival movements in India such as the Brahmo Samaj, which developed a close relationship with the American Unitarian movement. It was a great scandal when a Baptist missionary converted to the Brahmo Samaj during that time. In 1878, the co-founder of the Theosophical Society, Henry Steele Alcott, converted to Buddhism in a public ceremony in Colombo, Ceylon, saying that he hoped the effects of that act had been transmitted across the Great Divide to his Puritan ancestors.

American Historical Scholarship on pre-Modern India

Burton Stein

Contributions by Americans to the understanding of India in the age before the advent of European imperialism have been substantial, both in quality and in quantity, when the relatively few scholars who have been committed to this research is considered. To the social histories of Bengal, Maharashtra and Tamil Nadu especially, American scholars have made contributions that have influenced some of the history writing practiced in India as well as in Europe; the work of others on political and religious history of the pre-modern era in the Deccan and elsewhere has attained the same high standing. Notwithstanding these accomplishments, the contributions of American scholars have done little to alter the views of even educated Americans about India, nor have they changed an Indian historiography that has been set by a twentieth century interaction.between the prevailing imperialist and nationalist interpretations of the Indian past.

This observation should prompt neither surprise nor dismay, since academic practitioners of history in the United States have marched to other drums—have followed other agendas—having to do with ideologically framed conceptions of the uniqueness of the American experience that has consistently sought to differentiate the American past from those of others in the world. Few have made more of this presumed uniqueness than the present Librarian of Congress, Daniel Boorstin. This insular and myopic characteristic of history in America has surely made the task of changing educated Americans' views of India difficult.

The self-imposed and ideologically constructed solipsism within academic history in the U.S. has been reflected in the composition of most university history departments where, to a major core of scholars of the American past, exquisitely graded temporally and thematically, were added specialists in European national histories in virtual conformity with the immigration quotas of the various nations from which the citizenry of twentieth century America originated. Before World War II, this means principally from Britain and Western Europe. After 1950, except in a few east coast universities that bred diplomats and missionaries, Asian historians were added to history faculties, less from any quickened interest or curiosity about Asia than from the new role of the U.S. as a world power with perceived interests in Asia. Not surprisingly, early Indian history was not considered a very important field of research and instruction in its own right, and the small attention and support that has been given to it has come from within area studies programs on India. These programs have provided the context for most of the academic work in India over the past two decades and for the modest attention given to pre-modern history.

The core and ultimate reason for being of area studies programs in the U.S. has been to provide training in Indian languages. For a time, when resources were abundant, each area studies center strove to offer tuition in as many of the modern languages of the subcontinent as it could under an operating logic that each center in each university should be complete in itself with respect to the training of any of its students and to maximize its receipt of subvending funds under the National Defense Education Act. Instruction in Sanskrit was included as well, partly because Sanskritists were often the only members of faculties at many of the universities at which area studies were first introduced, partly because of the influence of such eminent Sanskritists as W. Norman Brown in establishing these programs and partly as a proposed means for students of India to access the foundations of contemporary cultures of India and thus of understanding the cultural contexts in which contemporary Indians are presumed to have lived their lives and used their modern languages. India's pre-modern past was slotted into the same utilitarian structure, to provide an appreciative understanding of India's pre-colonial past when the living cultural traditions of the present age were presumably formed and fixed.

History departments of most of the universities where area studies programs were launched during the 1960s were persuaded to appoint young scholars with degrees in Indian history—most in modern history—by the provision of part of their salaries from area studies center budgets and by the successful lobbying for more undergraduate courses in non-Western history, or, more grandiosely, "civilization" (as if there were only one such marked category). Most history departments were delighted to have the salary subventions and the additional history department enrollments, and most departments saw nothing deficient in young colleagues with degrees in modern Indian history teaching about the pre-modern past, though most would have objected to any such arrangement in, say, British or German history.

None of this should be construed as denigrating the accomplishments of Indian area studies programs severally or collectively. Their stimulation to training and research in the major modern Indian languages and in classical languages was unprecedented, and the effects of this upon American universities will be long-lasting. The same is true in fields such as history, philosophy, religion, art and art history, and in comparative literature. But, against these substantial achievements in and for American higher education—its teaching, its research and its libraries—must be set some costs and also some considerations for the future.

Among the chief costs have been to those social scientists who have been involved in the Indian area studies enterprise. Political scientists, sociologists, economists and economic historians and social historians who have participated in the area-oriented "packaging" of Indian studies in the U.S. have by now, in most cases, either lost contact with their respective social science colleagues or they have left the substantive Indian field of research and teaching. We often fail to recognize that one sort of contrast between the scholars in humanities fields and social scientists is that, within the humanist canon, concentration by a scholar upon one diverse and rich civilization such as India has always been considered an adequate epistemological base for the generation of new and significant knowledge to any field of humanistic learning. No such notion of adequacy has been recognized for social scientists, however, and comparisons across fundamentally different cultural domains continues to be posited as important for social scientific analysis. To epistemology has been added the principled apperception by social scientists that most of the world's societies have been, are and will continue to be involved in world-wide economic, political, social and cultural processes which make any single one a questionable source for the kind of generalized formulations which it is the intention—if not always the practice—of social scientists to strive to frame.

During the 1950s and 1960s, "modernization theory" appeared to provide such a comparative framing for any problem addressed by the social scientist in India. According to that theory, all non-Westernized societies were in an implied comparative relation with a generalized, super society called "The West," the "developed" or "first" world, whose "modernization" was the mimicked future of "backward" societies like India. This false, crude and arrogant presumption of modernization theory has been recognized in the last decade and castigated for what it is, but this has left most policy-oriented social scientists who also remain Indianists with little valid ground upon which to base their knowledge. Those that did not become deans have tended to escape into history where the comparative element has never been so demanding.

The one social science that has thrived until the present is anthropology. If there has been a hegemonic discourse among American students of Indian society—pre-modern as well as modern—it has been anthropology. Its method of participant observation of seemingly simple, rural peoples appeared to fit the perceived sociological realities of "village India," and its variant form in the U.S.—cultural anthropology—seemed apt for apprehending India's cultural principles, its hierarchies and its unities. Now, alas, even American anthropologists of India confront an intellectual crisis not unlike that of colleagues in the other social sciences. For, notions about village isolates and consistent social relations of hierarchy seem to be fictitious, chimera thrown around presumed characteristics of Indian societies that mask quite other and determining forces emanating from large and small urban places, from deliberately interventionist bureaucracies and from an obdurately hostile and dangerous world beyond the subcontinent. The small-world methodology of anthropology has seemed ludicrously feeble against a canvas so broad and in societies whose self-knowledge is fortified by great and ancient literatures and tens of thousands of relevant texts.

To the chagrin of many humanist scholars of the pre-modern age and of many social scientists of India's more recent past, who cooperate together to staff the area studies programs on India, they find themselves accused of harboring orientalist conceptions. In the manner of orientalism everywhere in the world beyond Europe, Indian beliefs, customs, institutions have been set apart from those of the rest of humanity and they have been reduced to a set of essences. Such setting apart—an inferred, objectified "otherness"—and essentialism must ultimately degrade the Indian "object" as well as the American scholarly subject. Pre-modern scholars of India—those of humanities fields and those of the social sciences—are not exempt from this accusation. Along with their anthropologist colleagues (in the U.S. and elsewhere), they have too readily presumed attributes like caste, *jajmani* and hierarchy rather than showing whether and in what conditions these forms existed. The very designation of "traditional studies" contrasted to "modern studies" which was adopted for this symposium reflects the same sort of essentializing and objectifying that haunts our efforts at understanding, and on that account I have used the term "pre-modern" to designate a broad era before the categorizing hand of European commentators seized and held to fortune an Indian past.

If the collective crisis engendered by pervasive orientalism, by discredited modernization theory and Parsonian functionalism, its handmaiden, is as real as I believe it is for American scholars of India, then remedies must be sought. One that suggests itself is abandoning the area studies approach for the study of India. There are several reasons for proposing this drastic step. The first is that area studies programs have achieved the major objectives of having made the study of India a legitimate pursuit in many American universities, and have helped, by external funding, to add to the faculties of these universities scholars competent to teach and guide research of American students on a wide variety of Indian subjects. The prospects of adding substantially to this institutional development is too obviously poor—and has been for some years—to anticipate more of such development, even if that were thought desirable. Secondly, the area studies approach has not resulted in any discernible enrichment of the various disciplines of humanistic or social science scholarship. Perhaps the opposite is more true. That is, American scholars of India have become encysted in their Indian programs and are increasingly ignored by departmental colleagues. Thus, rather than enriching the content of knowledge offered to these colleagues and to students in their fields, India has become ghettoized. Thirdly, there seems to be some thought and some lobbying to create what has been called a "National Endowment for Area Studies," presumably to provide secure and long-term funding for programs on India and other societies of the "Third World." This prolongation of "infant industry" status for Indian studies is unnecessary and only extends the ghettoized existence that Indian studies presently suffers. It is a proposal that requires very serious consideration and debate, not least because the achievement of a better understanding of India by Americans may be better served by other means, including direct support to undergraduate and graduate students.

DISCUSSION

This paper evoked a lengthy discussion of the virtues of the "area studies" concept with those present generally in favor of a cross-disciplinary approach to the South Asian studies curriculum. One suggestion was that the notion of area studies may be largely illusory, since South Asian teachers are typically lodged in disciplinary departments. Indianists invariably feel that it is impossible to study only one's own discipline and be any good as a scholar of India—language study is needed, and the interrelationship between fields, e.g. religion and anthropology, make courses in several disciplines essential. The speaker responded that there are many ways to study language and that language training can be centralized. He said that the fact that the Great-Little Tradition concept was brought in from folk-urban and Mexican anthropology illustrates the kind of fructifying that disciplines provide. But few would argue that in most academic departments, the Indianist is treated in the same way or is as completely integrated as his European or American counterpart. Often he is marginal as a political scientist, sociologist, historian or whatever. This may depend upon the field, to some extent. Literature and religion may compel more identity with a group of people than does history or economics, which may be more concerned with process.

Dr. Stein believes there is life after area studies if Indianists return to the framework that already exists; rejoin a kind of continuing and evolving discourse with colleagues that for most scholars probably has the richest intellectual meaning, whatever one's passion for India may be.

Other speakers saw the area studies concept as an archetype. The India faculty are typically few and diversified and in need of mutual support. They cannot claim a significant share of university funds because South Asia attracts relatively few students. You get a language teacher instead of a department and language teaching materials and secondary materials on the literature which are relatively primitive—European languages get much more attention and institutional support. The classical tradition is rich, and Sanskritists are generally respected on campus; at some points of contact, e.g. Indian textual criticism, colleagues may find comparison intriguing. But without the anchor of area studies, could the other language and discipline courses long survive?

The Status of Medieval Hindi Studies in North America

Charles S.J. White

Let me say first of all that in my wildest imagination—after finishing my B.A. degree in English literature, let alone when I was chipping paint on the U.S.S. Tripoli on which I served during the Korean War—I could not have conjured up the possibility of earning my way through to the Ph.D. degree in the Divinity School of the University of Chicago by studying the Hindi language on government grants. But such was my fate for four years: Hindi, to which was added Sanskrit as well. I faced the challenges that all students in the history of religions have, which is to combine study in systematic and methodological issues with a specialization that is in some sense technical: it need not, of course, be in Asian language and area studies, nor indeed in languages at all. I knew from the very start, however, that once I had committed myself to study Hinduism I would make a serious effort to adapt myself to living in India and using an Indian language. Hindi was, therefore, at the very least a means, but it also became an end in itself.

Circumstances contributed to my choice of the *bhakti* tradition in medieval Hinduism as an area of concentration. I came under the inspiring influences of Professor Shyam Manohar Pandey on the teaching staff in the South Asia Program of the University of Chicago, and the visits to Chicago of Professor Charlotte Vaudeville of the Sorbonne, the foremost Western scholar in the field of medieval Hindi studies. This led to my writing my dissertation on the subject, "Bhakti as a Religious Structure in the Context of Medieval Hinduism in the Hindi-Speaking area of North India."[1]

Although it is undoubtedly true that we were doing so, it did not occur to me at the time that those of us studying the Indian vernaculars were really pioneering in new fields within the American academy. I, also, was so naive as to think that being an American was not a major obstacle to what I was doing. Perhaps I was simply in shock in the first stages, too, of having begun to study Sanskrit! In the fields of esoteric (from the Western point of view) literary languages, it has not been as common for Americans to develop magisterial competence as it has been for Europeans, with a traditional education in classics and several modern Western languages. Of course, there are exceptions. We cannot discount sheer chance in the novel situation of Americans being trained in the Indian vernaculars. What was it in the early 1960s that brought about the sudden discovery by the American government that there was a critical shortage of individuals competent in unusual languages that might have strategic importance? And then, why has so little been done about it since? I have extracted a bit of wry comfort over the years from the thought, as I labor in the mines of Washington, D.C. academic life, that I am a kind of stockpiled resource, waiting only the right moment to be dusted off and rushed to the front lines of civilization. I am like cheese that could be taken from a refrigerated warehouse if the government could only figure out a moral way to dispense it to those who need it. As it is, once competent, I gradually became twice forgotten.

Nevertheless, there have been some compensations. I have found my visits to India much more worthwhile because I can use the Hindi language well enough to work independently of translators or English speakers, both in the conduct of research and in the affairs of daily life. It is rewarding, too, to see that Indian scholars are pleased that an American has made some progress in mastering the Hindi language. Practically speaking, I am certain that I speak for the community of Hindi scholars in expressing gratitude for the support given by the American Institute of Indian Studies and the Smithsonian Institution. Both these organizations have generously funded the study of scholars whose work on Indian languages is understood for its intrinsic value. Academic publishers, particularly, have generously brought writings in this area to the attention of the public.

The group of those Americans who share any degree of training in the field of medieval Hindi studies is small. When I began my studies, there were very few of us and we grasped for proper approaches. Some of the new wave of scholars are doing excellent work in synthetic interpretations of important areas of the several genres of medieval Hindi and in creditable translations and literary criticism. Those of us who studied Indian languages in the South Asian program at Chicago owe a special debt of gratitude to Professor Edward Dimock and Professor Norman Zide, who taught and encouraged us in their distinct ways and who have been our friends and colleagues since then.

The history of Hindi poetry goes back to before the Muslim period and includes examples in more than one dialect. The sixteenth century was a time of considerable efflorescence in the Braj Bhāṣā and Awadhi dialects, the former the language of many works about Kṛṣṇa and the latter especially important because of the beauty and widespread influence of Tulsī Dās's *Rāmāyaṇa*. Most contemporary American scholars of the Hindi middle ages have chosen to work on the writers who are best known and that have engaged the greatest interest of Indian scholars who write about their own literary heritage. This is understandable and allows the American scholar to immediately enter into the discussion with leading European and Indian critics. This is according to a pattern already established by Charlotte Vaudeville and Hugh McLeod abroad. A further advantage is that the text is fairly well-established because of the work of recent generations of Indian scholars. This leaves one free in some cases to deal with more exquisite issues. Of course, establishing a text from prior to the modern period is bound to remain a somewhat open issue.

Among the pioneers in the field in this country is Professor Usha Saksena Nilsson, who works on the poet Mīrā Bāī. Professors Norman Zide and S.M. Pandey also worked on Mīrā Bāī. There are several North American scholars who have published book-length studies relevant to the most highly regarded Braj poet, Sūrdās. Professor Kenneth E. Bryant published a solid introduction to aspects of Sūr's work in 1978. It was entitled, *Poems to the Child God* (The University of California Press), and included selections from the corpus of Sūrdās in Bryant's own very good translation, together with literary-critical apparatus. It is not a complete translation of Sūrdās. Professor Norvin J. Hein's *The Miracle Plays of Mathura*, published by Yale in 1972 was the first such major work on the Rās Līlā dramas by an American and has been followed by Professor John S. Hawley's *At Play With Krishna* (Princeton, 1981), which includes vivid translations from the Rās Līlā drama. Professor Hawley has published a study of Krishna as *Krishna, the Butter Thief* (Princeton, 1983), and *Sūr Dās: Poet, Singer, Saint* (University of Washington Press, 1984). Professor Hawley's work is rich in nuances and is all the more effective because of his engaging English style.

Another publication is important among the pieces produced by North Americans on the Hindi materials of the Vallabhite tradition. This is the work of Professor Richard Barz, likewise a disciple of Professor S.M. Pandey. His work is entitled *The Bhakti Sect of Vallabhacarya* (Delhi, 1976). Part II of that publication contains a translation of the *Caurāsī Vaiṣṇavam kī Varta,* which is so important in establishing the context of the devotional life in medieval Braj. My own article, "Kṛṣṇa as a divine child," published in *History of Religions* in 1970, included samples from the *Sūr Sāgar* and was drawn from my dissertation of 1964.[2] The translation

I did of the *Caurāsī Pad* of Srī Hit Harivams (University of Hawaii Press, 1977) was, I believe, the first full-length translation into a European language of that author's principal Hindi work.[3]

Other recent research in medieval Hindi, either published or in process or in dissertation includes Dr. Barron Gregory Holland's "The *Satsaī* of Bihārī: Hindi poetry of the Early Period," a dissertation presented to the University of California in 1969. Phillip Lutgendorf's "The Life of a Text" (on the *Rāmcaritmānas* of Tulsīdās) was a Ph.D. dissertation at the University of Chicago in 1986. Linda Hess published *The Bījak of Kabīr* (San Francisco, North Point Press, 1983). Professor David Lorenzen's work on Kabir legends is in process. Daniel Gold and Ann Gradson Gold's *The Lord as Guru in North Indian Religion*, a study of the Nāth Sampradāy, an important religious group, that contributes to our understanding of certain literary movements of the classical Hindi period, is forthcoming from Oxford University Press.[4]

The study of medieval Hindi cannot be divorced from the work of American Sanskritists, who treat later materials of that language related to the *bhakti* movement. It is not possible to mention many of them here, but Professor Frances Wilson's translation of the *Kṛṣṇacaraṇāmṛta* (University of Pennsylvania Press, 1975) was a landmark. The recent work of Professor James Redington as an interpreter of the refinements of Vallabhite theology through his close association with Vallabha sectarians, published in *Vallabhācārya on the Love Games of Kṛṣṇa* (Motilal Banarsidass, 1983), will add considerably to our ability to interpret the Braj materials generally, as well as Sūrdās and similar poets in particular. Barbara Stoler Miller's *Love Song of the Dark Lord: Jayadeva's Gītagovinda* (Columbia University Press, 1977) contains one of the most beautiful translations ever done from an Indian language into English and perfectly captures the refined ardor of *bhakti* mysticism. Wendy Doniger O'Flaherty's works of interpretation of the Sanskrit corpus enlighten various aspects of later developments in the tradition.

In conclusion, I must admit to a sense of frustration when thinking about how I and others must carry out our work in medieval Hindi studies. The American Institute of Indian Studies and the Smithsonian Institution, together, perhaps, with the Fulbright fellowships program, have made it all possible, indeed have been indispensable. Since publishing the work mentioned earlier, I undertook a season (actually eighteen months in its entirety) of fieldwork in India in 1983-84 sponsored by Smithsonian, in which I directed a microfilming project aimed at conserving the manuscripts and rare books of a cross-section of the Vaisnava canons, both vernacular and Sanskrit, in south India as well as north India. Although it is at present suspended, hopefully not indefinitely, an aspect of that experience might be relevant to our discussions here.[5]

The atomized character of American universities with their very diverse orientations and commitments to area studies in general, or Indian area studies or Indology in particular, combined with government capriciousness, does not allow one to plan for very long term commitments to work in the field in India. (I mean to include also the creation of a stable system of associates, pandits, bibliographical and philological colleagues in India and the like, with whom one could cooperatively bring to fruition the great potential remaining for work in medieval Hindi studies. One might compare for instance the opportunity afforded our French colleagues through the Ecole francaise d'Extreme Orient.) However, I learned from the microfilming experience that it is possible, as we did with the Vrindavan Research Institute, to establish a common framework of teamwork oriented toward a useful common goal—the preservation of an endangered literature, endangered because of the continuing destruction of manuscripts and the paucity of interest in the preservation of manuscripts, with the aim in mind of doing definitive editions, annotations, commentaries, translations and the like. The Vrindavan Research Institute has an international character to it and might well serve as a focus for an enterprise directed toward the production of a series of works on our subject area in cooperation with the international community of Hindi scholars. The need is great, the American commitment pitifully small. The help received on an *ad hoc* basis from AIIS, Fulbright and Smithsonian have made what has been accomplished possible. I do believe that for those of us in this area of study, discovering a common base for cooperation in an organization like the Vrindavan Research Institute, or even a base maintained in some fashion in North America, could add impetus to the favorable beginning we have made in making a less well-known aspect of the Indian experience available to English readers of North America and elsewhere.

DISCUSSION

Discussion of the area studies concept resumed, led by Dr. Rudolph. Her view was that there are no universalist answers to the issues being discussed. Curricula on India differ from one university to another, one program to another, and some teaching departments are clearly more hospitable to

South Asian courses than are others. Interdisciplinary courses have worked very well at Chicago without compromising the disciplinary interests of participating faculty. The notion that powerful theory and analysis can be derived only from traditional disciplines is patently erroneous and invests them with more authority than they deserve. It is important to get outside one's discipline from time to time as well as to bring something back to it. Moreover, area studies centers are visible units that provide support for a network of teaching positions and courses that might be individually vulnerable to a predatory provost or dean. They invest the program with a certain amount of institutional durability. Dr. Stein replied that the traditional departments are the responsibility of their members and must be nourished to provide a congenial home. You get back what you put into them. External support is fragile and we can't plan well for the future by running one step ahead of the bloke with the broom. Dr. O'Flaherty noted that in Chicago, at least, one can move back and forth between Center and Department according to current concerns or obligations. In the best of all possible worlds, one should not have to choose one or the other.

Dr. Ramusack spoke as the only Indian specialist at the University of Cincinnati; she has no area studies refuge in which to talk shop with area specialist colleagues and must depend upon conferences like this one. One can, on the other hand, influence disciplinary colleagues over a period of time to take one's interests into account, whether it be Asia, women, or Asian women. Dr. O'Flaherty pointed out that in order for students to get jobs, they have to be trained in disciplines. But South Asianists need broader training than that and, as a result, often take two or three years longer than their fellows to finish their Ph.D.'s. That is a heavy price to pay. Dr. Hart wondered what the field would look like if there were not area studies programs. Would students learn Indian languages? Would they be likely to acquire the knowledge they need before going to India? How many students would there be likely to be?

NOTES

1. In the course of preparing that study, I consulted a Ph.D. dissertation by W.C. MacDougall on the *Rāmāyaṇa* of Tulsīdās. It had been accepted for the doctor's degree at Chicago in 1926.
2. Recently, I had one of those happy experiences in our profession of discovering a translation I had done from Sufi Hindi poetry and published in an article in *History of Religions* in 1965 quoted in the recent work of Dr. Anne Marie Schimmel, entitled *And Mohammed is His Messenger* (University of North

Carolina Press, 1985). Among other things, its publication reminded me of an aspect of medieval Hindi literature on which Professor S.M. Pandey had done pioneering work and on which new work by American scholars would be very useful.

3. I owed something in the process to the redoubtable F.S. Growse's *Mathura: A District Memoir* (North-Western Provinces and Oudh Government Press, 1883), in which the first twelve stanzas of *Caurāsī Pad* had been translated. Reading these contributed to the ambition to complete the translation.
4. I am grateful to Professor Alf Hiltebeitel of George Washington University and Professor John S. Hawley of Columbia University for assistance in updating this summary of scholarship related to medieval Hindi.
5. I am grateful to the work of Professor Maureen Patterson in devising an expansive format for preserving the memory of the various writings of scholars in Indian studies. It is a great work by an American scholar, and I used it to help put together these comments: *South Asian Civilizations: A Bibliographic Synthesis* (Chicago, 1981).

Section III

CULTURAL INTERCHANGE AND AMERICAN PERCEPTIONS OF INDIAN CULTURE

American Understanding of Indian Art

Pramod Chandra

An acquaintance with Indian culture, particularly as it is expressed through religion and philosophy, began in the United States in the 1830s with the work of the New England Transcendentalists. There is evidence of this in the works of Ralph Waldo Emerson, Henry David Thoreau and their followers, but none of them appears to have considered Indian art in any of its manifestations.[1] While an interest in the religions and philosophy and also the languages and literature of India continued to develop during much of the nineteenth century, Indian art remained an untrodden field. No person seems to have systematically collected objects of art, even as curiosities, in spite of the increasing trade between the two countries, with Yankee merchants enjoying good profits in the exchange of goods, including ice from New England's ponds for Indian spices and animal hides.

One might have expected Charles Eliot Norton, who went to India for several months in 1849 and 1850 and who later served as a pioneering and distinguished professor of art at Harvard University, to have taken an interest in Indian art, but I have not yet been able to unearth any evidence that he did. At best, all that can be said of this early period of contact between India and the United States is that notwithstanding the lack of interest shown for art, a generally sympathetic atmosphere for things Indian was created by the Transcendentalists in the intellectual circles of New England, and there was no tradition of active hostility or repugnance toward Indian art, which continued to be the common attitude in England and, to a lesser extent, Europe, at the time.

It was only towards the end of the nineteenth century and during the first decade of the twentieth century that things began to change in America. Once again, the center of activities was New England, this time Boston, where a concern for the arts of Asia, particularly those of Japan, was developing, if there was not much interest in the art of India itself. Edward Sylvester Morse, a naturalist who became fascinated with Japanese art during a stay in that country during the 1880s, and Ernest Francisco Fenellosa, an American professor from Salem at Tokyo University, whose love for Japanese art and culture knew few limits, became avid collectors,

Fenellosa ending up by becoming a convert to Buddhism. The Morse collection and the Fenellosa collection both finally entered the Boston Museum with Fenellosa following as curator. Another important figure of this period was Okakura Kakuzo, belonging to a Japanese samurai family turned silk merchants. He was an associate of Fenellosa and was primarily responsible for the enactment of the National Treasures Law of 1884, which was designed to protect Japanese art and to prevent its indiscriminate export from the country. It is a testimony to the liberal temper of the times that Okakura also served as the advisor-curator of the Japanese collections at the Boston Museum of Fine Arts between 1904 and 1913, cataloging its collection of East Asian art. Okakura was a figure of international stature who took great pride in the Asian heritage as a whole. "Asia is one," he declared in ringing tones after a year's visit to India in 1901 and 1902, "the Himalayas divide only to accentuate two mighty civilizations ..., but not even the snowy barriers can interrupt for one moment that broad expanse of love for the Ultimate and Universal which is the common thought-inheritance of every Asian race."[2] Okakura was a friend of Swami Vivekananda who had given a stirring address on Hinduism to the Parliament of World Religions held at Chicago in 1893, the year of the Columbian Exposition. He also developed a certain intimacy with Rabindranath Tagore. A visit to the famous cave temples of Ajanta in western India is recorded by Sister Nivedita, an associate of Vivekananda,[3] and one can be reasonably certain of his admiration for the art of India for he expressed great regret at what had been effaced by invasions. This did not translate, however, into any acquisitions of Indian art for the Boston Museum.

Acquisition was left to yet another Bostonian, Denman W. Ross, Lecturer in the Theory of Design at Harvard University from 1899 to 1935, a man of substantial means, an art collector of great generosity, and a trustee of the Boston Museum. We do not know how he developed a taste for Indian miniature painting, but it would be fair to surmise, I think, that this was an outgrowth of his great appreciation for oriental art, particularly Japanese prints with their drawing in outline and painting in flat tones. We thus see him strongly supporting the purchase in 1914 of Victor Goloubew, a Russian emigre living in Paris who had fine examples of Mughal and Persian painting. This acquisition seems to have been made, partly at least, through the good offices of Ananda Kentish Coomaraswamy, a person who was to play a dominant part both in the understanding of Indian art in America and in this lecture. Coomaraswamy, of English and Sri Lankan parentage, was somewhere in his mid-1930s, and, at the time, maintained a residence in England. The meeting of Denman Ross and Ananda Coomaraswamy was, as we shall shortly describe, of great significance for the study, scholarship and awareness of Indian art in America. It led, relatively quickly, to the acquisition in 1917 of Coomaraswamy's unique collection of Indian art, primarily of miniature painting, by the Boston Museum of Fine Arts through the generosity of Ross. It also led, and this is even more important, to the acquisition of Coomaraswamy himself as keeper of a separate department of Indian art at the Boston Museum. This was for its time a startling development, for few museums in the Western world thought enough of Indian art to give it this kind of recognition.

With Ananda Coomaraswamy's arrival in Boston in 1917, the foundations for the study of Indian art in America began to be well and truly laid, for Coomaraswamy soon developed into what I consider to be the greatest scholar of Indian art of this century. America and the Boston Museum of Fine Arts can take much credit for this, supporting the preservation and display of Indian art and its serious study in a major way at a time when Coomaraswamy had tried desperately to find a home for his collection in an Indian museum and had struggled also for the establishment of a national museum in that country, but to no avail. It was left to the Boston Museum, with its tradition of sympathetic study of the arts of China and Japan, to add a new dimension to its achievements by promoting this fresh understanding of Eastern art in America and, for that matter, the Western world. To Coomaraswamy himself, this new receptive atmosphere of encouragement and understanding must have been a startling change from the continuing, if weakening, hostility and opposition of England and Europe to the art of India, of which he was so pugnacious a champion.

With the wisdom of hindsight, Coomaraswamy's arrival in the United States can now be regarded as the first step in a process by which the United States replaced Europe as the leading center for the study of Indian art. I am, therefore, prompted to go into the career of this remarkable man in some detail, for the understanding of Indian art in America has been to a great extent bound up with him, and I doubt if we would be where we are had it not been for his indefatigable scholarship. Born in 1877 in Sri Lanka, and forty years of age when appointed to the Boston Museum of Fine Arts, Coomaraswamy already had an extraordinary career behind him both as a scholar and what we would call an activist fighting for Indian culture. Much of his childhood and youth was spent in England, where he acquired a typical British education in public school. In college, he specialized in geology, returning to Sri Lanka in 1902 at the age of 25 to become director of the Mineralogical Survey of Ceylon. There he was deeply affected by what he called the ruin of native life and manners before advancing modern and Western civilization, a feeling which led him to a sensitive study of the threatened arts and crafts of India and Sri Lanka. From this, the transition to the history of their art was a natural step, as was a fierce and unrelenting opposition to those forces which he saw as destructive of traditional cultures.

Leaving Sri Lanka in 1907, he spent the next decade both in India and in England. In India, he became a fervent nationalist and a strong advocate of the preservation of national culture as a part of the struggle against British imperialism. In England, he was deeply influenced by the Arts and Crafts Movement, and became a leading defender of the ideals of Indian art against the wanton attacks heaped upon it. He was one of the principal founders, in 1910, of the India Society, which was formed by a group of influential English artists including William Rothenstein and Roger Fry after a particularly outrageous public remark by Sir George Birdwood, an English civilian, to the effect that a boiled suet pudding was as expressive of passionate purity and serenity of soul as a Buddha image.[4]

All of his involvement in the active life, however, did not come in the way of Coomaraswamy's undertaking a keen and critical study of the history of art, particularly that of Asia and India, and a passionate drive to preserve what he could from destruction. In the course of these pursuits, he was able to bring together a sizeable collection, notably of neglected and unstudied miniature paintings, later identified by him as works of a separate Rajput school (as distinct from Mughal) in an epoch-making book published in 1916.[5] Much of this collecting activity was inspired by Coomaraswamy's total involvement, for a while, in the setting up of an art section in the United Provinces exhibition held at the city of Allahabad in the winter of 1910-11. It was Coomaraswamy's hope that this exhibition would lead to the establishment of an art museum in India which would house his collection with him as curator, but these hopes, as I have just said, were belied. In 1912, we find him again in England with his unique, if not greatly appreciated collection. During the next four years, he seems to have concentrated on research, writing and publishing a number of important books and articles on Indian art and religion, and it was during this time that he seems to have first come into contact with Denman Ross.

The details of Coomaraswamy's relationship with Ross are not yet known, but I suspect there must have been a meeting of minds, for they certainly shared several ideas in common. Both were scornful of so-called "original genius," and the whole idea of art as primarily a matter of self-expression, both of them believing that true art follows principles and is governed by rules. Ross was also much interested in the arts of China and Japan, particularly admiring the Japanese for what he called their unsurpassed love of excellence and perfection.[6] It might be fair to assume that Ross's views on these matters spilled over into an interest in Indian art. The Boston Museum had already become a center of a new appreciation of Asian art under the curatorship of Fenellosa and Okakura; the Goloubew collection of Indian and Persian painting had already been acquired with the help of Ross, and the acquisition of Coomaraswamy's collection and his move to Boston was to be expected. William Rothenstein, the English painter and principal of the Royal School of Art, later remarked that "Coomaraswamy's sympathies with the vision of the Indian nationalists caused him to loosen his ties with England, and America has had the benefit of his wide scholarship and understanding."[7] As I mentioned at the beginning of this lecture and would now repeat, I find myself in agreement with Rothenstein that the importance of Coomaraswamy's arrival in Boston to the introduction and study of Indian art in the United States must not be underestimated. With this move to America of a pre-eminent scholar in those days when the serious study of Indian art itself was a relatively rare phenomenon, the United States became an extremely important and arguably the leading center for the study of Indian art.

Coomaraswamy quickly settled down to work in his new home and from his desk poured numerous writings that gave the study of Indian art a very different aspect than it previously possessed, reconstructing its long history and explaining its meaning in a profound and convincing manner. I do not propose to go into detail about these achievements here, for they are, more or less, universally acknowledged. For the present purpose, it would perhaps be sufficient to draw attention to the contemporary *Catalogue* in five volumes of the Boston collection, the first of its kind for Indian art; the *History of Indian and Indonesian Art*, a work unsurpassed as a work of reference; the monograph in two parts on *Yaksas*; a book on *Elements of Buddhist Iconography*, which tackled problems of meaning in a fundamental way; and an essay on the *Origin of the Buddha Image*, which is a classic contribution to a perplexing theme in the history of Indian art and to studies of origins of themes and motifs in art in general.[8] These and much more poured from Coomaraswamy's active pen. But here I must move ahead.

What should be of greater interest to the audience assembled here and pertinent to the subject of this symposium on the American understanding of India is the manner in which Coomaraswamy addresses the general problems involved in comprehending the art of India by other, outsiders or "foreigners," if we will, among whom he would have happily included those who, though they happened to be born in India, had lost contact with their traditional Indian culture, whether through training or by temperament or personal taste. It is the kind of problem that has never quite left us. In recent years, it has been once again coming to the fore despite a whole cycle of scholarship, even if in a different context and a different way. At a seminar on Understanding the Art of Others, held recently at Harvard University, my colleague Oleg Grabar, Aga Khan Professor of Islamic Art, referred, somewhat challengingly, I thought, to the current assumptions whereby the visual arts, like music, are thought to cut across linguistic, ethnic, national or cultural frontiers, as nothing but a common cliche of our time. And, by implication, the belief that anyone who has the inclination or desire to do so may obtain some aesthetic, sensuous or intellectual satisfaction from seeing and presumably learning about any work of art or architecture is also considered a cliche. This view, it was asserted, contrasts to the approach to poetry, where understanding and appreciation, it is generally believed, requires the profound knowledge of a language and of the culture, perhaps even of the cultural moment, that produces it. As I listened to Professor Grabar, I remembered that questions of this type and the possible answers had been anticipated by Ananda Coomaraswamy some fifty years ago. Regarding the relationship between poetry and the other arts, he was fond of quoting Plato to the effect that all arts are a kind of poetry. As for the possibility of sensuous satisfaction, Coomaraswamy believed that it was the least of our problems, for every work of art could most surely excite some sensuous feelings in those who wished to be so stimulated. Thus, there well could be persons who are excited or stunned by the sheer sounds of a particular work of poetry even though they do not understand any word of it. It may not be much, but they are getting something out of it. On the other hand, if they understood the language and the culture in which the poetry was produced, they would not only receive sensory enjoyment but much more. And this greater understanding would be sure to affect and even refine the sensual response experienced initially. Similarly, with works of visual art, Coomaraswamy pointed out, one gets as much out of an object or a painting as one puts into it. The work of art, he asserted, yields its meaning at different levels to different persons, depending upon their own inner capabilities and, by implication, their preparation. This, Coomaraswamy demonstrated, was a proposition not different from what prevailed in ancient India, judging from the reactions to art that had been preserved in the literature of the country. Thus, the ordinary layman would be pleased by the bright color or impressed by the sheer virtuosity of execution; artisans would appreciate the general technical skill; connoisseurs would be moved by the expression of mood and would be inclined to express their appreciation in technical terminology, or what many of you and some of us now call scholarly jargon; the religious would be interested in the representation of sacred themes as such; scholars would be concerned about the accuracy of provenance, historicity and iconography; and the pious would use works of art as a support for ultimate enlightenment. There was indeed a hierarchy in all of these levels of understanding, but none could be dismissed as unworthy *per se*. How, for example, could one criticise a person unacquainted with the norms of art for only being excited by the color and dextrousness of execution of the paintings of Ajanta? Difficulties arise, Coomaraswamy argued, if it is felt that this kind of sensuous enjoyment is the only way, or the best way, of understanding the paintings. The work of art, on the other hand, is to be thought of, according to a popular Indian image, as a *kāmadhenu*, a wish-fulfilling cow, yielding to the spectator precisely what he is capable of "milking" from it by virtue of his or her preparation or knowledge.[9] The ideal and complete understanding, of course, comes to one who has equipped himself with learning, piety perhaps, sensibility, a knowledge of technique and, indeed, the naive and innocent approach of the folk.

This faith that outsiders, if well-prepared, could properly understand the art of India always stayed with Coomaraswamy. At the same time, however, he never ceased to object strongly against what he called "aesthetes," who, according to him, are satisfied that a tingling of the nerve end is an index to understanding. The art of other peoples and ages, he pleaded, is to be understood "not by our aesthetic, but by their rhetoric," to use a favorite phrase; but an understanding is surely possible.

A concern with what constitutes true understanding led Coomaraswamy to question what he called the very special and historically provincial viewpoint of Western scholarship, in which he included Indian scholarship adopting Western methods. These, he believed, stressed essentially problems of style, chronology, attribution and so on. Useful and essential as these studies are at a certain level, it is a delusion to think that they in any real way contribute to the understanding of the art itself. Coomaraswamy thus began to question the whole procedure, to ask the kinds of questions that we seem to be again asking today. Witness, for example, the round table on the subject Western Methods and Eastern Art at the

1983 session of the International Congress of Art Historians held at Vienna. When Coomaraswamy wrote, the discipline seems hardly to have had the doubts that it appears to have now, so little attention was paid to his arguments. Perhaps this is an appropriate time to raise them again, as they may help us at the very least to formulate the proper questions, or they may at least indicate the direction from which significant answers might come.

Coomaraswamy began by rejecting the differentiation between fine and applied art, and in this he was doubtless influenced by the Arts and Crafts Movement to which he had been exposed in his youth. This was also a distinction for which he found no justification in the Indian texts. The Indian artist, he affirmed in one of his aphoristic statements, was not a special kind of man, but every man was a special kind of artist. He was simply a kind of expert, like a modern engineer. This being the case, the Indian artist saw no necessity to "express himself." True, every artist perforce leaves traces of his personality in what he creates, "just as the imperfections of an ax leave corresponding marks on the wood, so also does every period leave its imprint on its monuments." These, however, do not constitute the essence of the work and are really, according to Coomaraswamy, its accidents. To study the essence of an art, he was never tired of urging, we must place ourselves at the standpoint of those by and for whom the art was made; in other words, study it in terms of its own intentions.

A belief in the power of persuasion, which never quite left him, compelled Coomaraswamy, in addition to his scholarly work, to write essays aimed at the general audience, like those brought together in *The Dance of Shiva*, one of his most popular books, first published in 1918 and reprinted in 1924, 1957 and later as well. He also prepared a large introductory volume for the Boston Museum *Catalogue* aimed as much at the general public as others. His scholarly work, filled with vast learning, citing texts from several languages and written in an extremely terse and condensed style, was not the kind to be easily understood, and it was as if to compensate for this that he regularly lectured to lay audiences, including a series of radio broadcasts in 1937. From the end of World War I to the end of World War II, his was the most important voice attempting to promote the understanding of Indian art and culture in the United States.

"However uncompromising his rhetoric, he wanted to persuade,"[10] and his principal success was in learned and academic circles. In these he developed strong and sympathetic associations with several scholars, including some who had little interest in India or Indian art. Whether they agreed with his views and theories or not, they were willing to listen and argue, his erudition and integrity being broadly respected. As a result, Indian art, alongside Coomaraswamy, won an easy and almost imperceptible acceptability. Coomaraswamy's influence, not unexpectedly, was strongest in the Boston area. John Ellerton Lodge, Curator of Oriental Art both at the Boston Museum and the Freer Gallery, and Langdon Warner, Benjamin Rowland and Eric Schroeder, all at Harvard, being close admirers, through them and their students many of his ideas percolated to others. Outside Boston, it was Professor Meyer Schapiro of Columbia University with whom Coomaraswamy had taken issue on some points in a review of Arthur Upham Pope's *Survey of Persian Art*, apparently beginning a friendship in which artistic discourse flourished greatly.[11] On Coomaraswamy's death, Schapiro eulogized him as "one of the luminaries of scholarship from whom we all have learned, and by the immense range of his studies and his persistent questioning of the accepted values, he gave us an example of intellectual seriousness rare among scholars today."[12] Richard Ettinghausen, professor at the University of Michigan and curator at the Freer Gallery of Art and Sherman E. Lee, curator at Seattle and later director of the Cleveland Museum of Art, also came to admire his work. Outside this group, all historians of art, Coomaraswamy developed close friendships with George Sarton, the historian of science and Robert Ulich, professor of education, both at Harvard. He was constantly in touch with Mircea Eliade and Heinrich Zimmer in Europe, both of whom were influenced by his work, and he continued his association with them when they migrated to the United States. Through these persons and others Coomaraswamy continued to exercise an important, if often unseen, influence on sections of American intellectual life and this was, no doubt, of great importance for the understanding of India.

Though Coomaraswamy had been an ardent collector of Indian art in his youth, the passion for objects was soon to leave him. His additions to the holdings of the Boston Museum were modest, but he was, nevertheless, successful in persuading other American museums to develop collections of Indian art. Among these can be mentioned the Metropolitan Museum of Art in New York, the Freer Gallery of Art in Washington, D.C., and smaller museums such as the Worcester Art Museum in Massachusetts and the Albright Art Gallery in Buffalo, New York. He also encouraged and supported the Indian art dealer Nasli Heeramaneck, who had established himself in the United States in the 1920s and whose skills and activities were very important in arousing interest and appreciation for Indian art among collectors and museums. Significant collections were also built by Dr. Laurence Sickman at the Nelson-Atkins Museum at Kansas City and by Dr. Richard Fuller in Seattle on the West Coast. Much was purchased at prices that make one envious, but sometimes works of art were acquired by lucky chance. I cannot resist recounting Langdon Warner's experience with the hall of a South Indian temple now in the Philadelphia Museum of Art. Hearing of forty to fifty unoopened crates belonging to the estate of a local lady which the museum could have if it carried them away, he discovered architectural remains of obvious antiquity. They had been intended for the lady's garden as some sort of exotic gazebo. This incident occurred sometime in the early twenties and gives us some idea not only of the unexpected pleasures of collecting, but also of the status of Indian art at that time.[13] Collections made in America from the 1920s to the 1940s were, on the whole, relatively modest. Their importance lay in keeping interest in Indian art alive and laying the foundations for what was to follow. I doubt very much if the present prosperous condition of American collections would have been possible if the groundwork had not been done during the period of Coomaraswamy.

Other than the work of Coomaraswamy, not much seems to have been done in the history of Indian art during the post-World War I years. Professor W. Norman Brown of the University of Pennsylvania followed up Coomaraswamy's early efforts by deepening our knowledge of the little-known school of western Indian painting; Professor Benjamin Rowland of Harvard University wrote an important work on the *Wall Paintings of Central Asia, India and Ceylon*, graced by a lengthy introduction by Coomaraswamy on the nature of Buddhist art. Professor Ludwig Bachhofer of the University of Chicago published his great book, *Early Indian Sculpture*, in 1929. In this work, he stressed the necessity of a careful study of the style apart from the subject matter, striking a different note from that of Coomaraswamy and thus creating new tools for the understanding of Indian art, which have, regrettably enough, not been utilized to the extent they deserved.[14]

Coomaraswamy died in 1947 at the age of seventy. With his death, an era filled with the excitement of new ideas and discoveries about Indian art and religion also seems to have ended. No appointment was made in his place at the Boston Museum, but his loss was alleviated to some extent by the appointment of Professor Stella Kramrisch of Calcutta University to the University of Pennsylvania in 1950. She was a scholar of distinction who had spent many years in India. In broad intellectual outlook, her work was compatible with that of Coomaraswamy. She had, however, not lost her zest for objects and under her stewardship were held some fine exhibitions, including one on the art of Nepal, another on the ritual art of tribe and village and finally, the superb *Manifestations of Shiva* held at Philadelphia some five years ago.

The ending of World War II, Indian independence from British rule in 1947 (Coomaraswamy died only a month later), and the emergence of the United States as the greatest world power, in whose best interest it was to advance knowledge among its people of hitherto neglected parts of the globe, led to a much wider expansion of programs of Asian studies, including the study of India. Primary attention was devoted to linguistic, economic, political and social studies, but some of the interest spilled over into Indian culture. As far as Indian art was concerned, this increasing awareness was first felt in the growth of collections, notably of Indian miniature painting. This is hardly surprising in view of the appreciation promoted by the excellent collections of the Boston Museum. Changes in Indian society and the power structure made collecting that much easier, the ruling princes and chiefs being quick to sell their holdings of traditional art, these apparently being among their more expendable possessions. The lead was taken by private American collectors, of whom there were hardly any in the pre-War years. Among the most notable of this post-War group, to name just a very few, are John Kenneth Galbraith, the American ambassador to India in the early 1960s, Stuart Cary Welch, Edwin Binney 3rd, and more recently William K. Ehrenfeld. Private collectors of Indian sculpture were rarer, the most important being the late John D. Rockefeller 3rd, Avery Brundage and Norton Simon. Museum collections also continued to grow; the Rockefeller, Brundage and Simon collections actually became in time museums open to the public. The Cleveland Museum of Art and the Los Angeles County Museum made spectacular gains and most museums with examples of Indian art also succeeded in enlarging their collections. As a result, it would not seem to me to be an exaggeration to say that the holdings of Indian art in the United States are not less significant than those of Europe, where objects have been accumulating over a much longer time.

Eloquent testimony as this is to the growth of interest in Indian art, one cannot ignore the tensions that have been caused. Assured that foreign collecting would lead to a denuding of cultural patrimony, the Parliament of India enacted a law prohibiting the export of antiquities except by permission of the government. The enormous disparity of wealth between India and the Western countries made this inevitable; in the good old days, even American students on fellowships in India were prosperous enough to outbid Indian museums and collectors, not to mention the wealthy

American collecting class. Nevertheless, in spite of the law, American collections continued to grow, and, though the proverbial smoking gun was often not in evidence, it was quite obvious that a substantial portion of objects abroad had reached their destination illegally and surreptitiously. The high prices available for works of art abroad had also led to other undesirable side effects, particularly the damage and defacement of monuments by unscrupulous and avaricious traffickers, so much so that the native art dealer, in league with collectors abroad, has become part of the Indian demonology, pilloried in newspapers and finally condemned to be one of the various kinds of stock villains inhabiting the popular Indian cinema. There can be no denying the bitter resentment and growing suspicion and distrust in India, rightly or wrongly, against foreign collectors, scholars or those who have an interest in Indian art. I personally believe that the situation, which has long been subterranean, is likely to surface one day, sooner rather than later, and, unless addressed carefully could, ironically enough, damage the very cause that serious collecting seeks to serve.

Accompanying this phenomenal expansion of art holdings has been a growing scholarly interest which has resulted in the serious teaching of Indian art at nearly a dozen universities. One of these, Harvard University, has a permanent chair endowed by a private citizen, Mr. George P. Bickford, exclusively for the teaching of Indian art. I have at present the honor of occupying this chair. The work done in America by professors, students and curators has rapidly led to a situation in which the United States can claim to be the leading world center for studies in Indian art except, perhaps, for India. There are signs of vigorous activity from coast to coast with a variety of subjects receiving close attention. There are, thus, meticulous and closely documented studies of individual periods, notably the Gupta and the Pala, as well as regional studies like those of eastern and western India. Individual sites such as the cave temples of Ajanta have been put under microscopic scrutiny, and Indian temple architecture, following Indian innovation, is being interpreted and analyzed in a fresh manner. The study of Indian miniature painting has been greatly advanced, particularly in the connoisseurship of the Mughal school, and questions of methodology are beginning to be addressed once again. All in all, we have a field of the most lively interest, with a range of approaches from the almost purely aesthetic to the almost purely contextual, full of energy, vitality and some controversy, which is as it should be. The drawbacks are relatively few and none, it would seem, which cannot be overcome with time. One that often comes to my mind is the absence of sufficient emphasis on a knowledge of languages. We would be hard put to think of students with advanced degrees in European art who lack a knowledge of at least two European languages; but students without a knowledge of even one Indian language are not so scarce. Not that there are no other problems to worry about. Jobs are few, several well-qualified young scholars being without work, and enrollments have been declining. Perhaps there has been some overexpansion at the expense of quality, but it seems to me that the study of Indian art is not going to die of attrition. The desirability of its study seems to be widely understood.

One particular development of great importance that needs special mention is the establishment in the 1960s of an American institution for the documentation and study of Indian art located at Varanasi in India. Founded as the American Academy of Benares, it is now the Center for Art and Archaeology of the American Institute of Indian Studies. It is a body designed to work in cooperation with Indian scholars and has a unique archive of well-documented and easily accessible photographs. Those who study the history of art know what a boon this can be. Among the projects which the Center is sponsoring is the *Encyclopedia of Indian Temple Architecture*, the first volume of which was published in 1983. This project is the happy result of Indian scholarship and American entrepreneurship, a product of deep learning bringing together vast amounts of new knowledge. It is the brain-child of Mr. M.A. Dhaky, the distinguished Indian scholar who conceived the entire project, planned out the details, worked out the elaborate classification and methodology, determined the norms of presentation, assembled the staff, selected and persuaded the contributors, is himself a leading contributor and continues to work for the project up to the present day. The administrative framework, editorial assistance and the cost of the project have been largely provided by the Smithsonian Institution through the American Institute of Indian Studies. Here is a case of knowledge primarily possessed by Indian scholars surfacing with American help and know-how to the benefit of all scholarship and contributing to the training of American scholars as well. A signal service is being performed and I am quite sure that other joint enterprises of this type with even greater American scholarly contributions will develop in the future as the tempo of work accelerates in this country. Progress is impossible, however, without Indian cooperation. It is their art and most of the materials are and will continue to be there.

Special exhibitions are a well-known device for arousing public interest and though I can recall none of any importance in the United States in the years before Indian independence, there have been several thereafter. The exhibition of Indian sculpture sponsored by the Cleveland Museum of Art and some other museums in 1964 and 1965 was among the most important; the Philadelphia Museum's *Manifestations of Shiva*, which attempted to explore the meaning and significance of a major Hindu divinity, was perhaps the most unique.[15] All these culminated in the several exhibitions which formed part of the Festival of India, jointly sponsored by the Governments of India and the United States, an event inaugurated in 1985 and now drawing to a close. It has long been felt in India that even though the knowledge of Indian art and culture has been growing in the United States over the years, it was confined largely to a relatively small, if widening circle. The purpose of the Festival was to enthuse this circle and, more important, to put Indian achievements past and present before a much wider audience. With this aim, a busy schedule of events was planned, the lead being taken by a series of exhibitions including some major ones devoted to Indian art, and also extensive programs of music and dance, poetry and literature, films, seminars, lectures and other such activities. Mr. Ted Tanen, one of our panelists, who is intimately associated with the administration of the Festival of India, will, no doubt, be referring to it in greater detail. I will confine myself to saying just a few words about the art exhibitions. The first to open was arranged by the National Gallery of Art in Washington, D.C., and stressed the beauty and variety of Indian sculpture, displaying some of the choicest works of art ever to be seen outside of India. This was followed by the Metropolitan Museum of Art's sumptuous show of Indian miniature painting and the decorative arts in New York; and there were yet others devoted to Kushan sculpture, Akbar's India, the art of the courts, handicrafts, modern painting, ancient manuscripts and even the costumes of the maharajas, one after the other, the last in the series being the exhibition at San Francisco setting forth the classical subject matter of Indian art. Most of these exhibitions were accompanied by extensive catalogs that sold briskly and the attendance was very high, of a magnitude not seen before at exhibitions concerned with things Indian.[16] The interest evoked was indeed very great and the attention received in the news media was without precedent. All this activity inspired many American institutions to do what they could as a part of the general celebration, displaying their own collections which may have been in storage, and holding exhibitions of local scope. Among these were many museums that had no particular interest in India. I especially recall an evening in Framingham, not far from Boston, where the town museum had decided to put up a small exhibit of British prints depicting scenes from India. The accompanying lecture drew a capacity crowd; there were more people present than one would have ever expected in the old days. Though the long-range effect of the Festival cannot be presently gauged, there is little doubt in my mind that general American understanding and awareness of India has taken a great step forward.

Before closing, a few last remarks about the lingering survival of a hoary stereotype of complacent, self-congratulatory and thoughtlessly prejudiced mentality towards Indian art that has a well-documented history which goes back at least a century in the West. The development of this mentality, a natural enough product of its time, forms the subject of an important book by Partha Mitter, and with this, I would have thought, the devil would have been exorcised.[17] But no. So deeply ingrained are these that in spite of all our efforts, they unexpectedly appear, like genetic throwbacks, and without seeming cause, their very appearance being a matter of intellectual interest. The author of such ideas thinks that he is being clever, original, thoughtful and profound, but in reality he is being nothing of the kind, and has fallen victim, consciously or unconsciously, to the pattern of times long gone and past. I am referring, as some of you may have guessed, to an odd article that appeared, astonishingly enough, in *Commentary*, a New York intellectual magazine of some respectability that ever so modestly advertises itself as the most influential in America.[18]

When the article first came to my attention, my reaction was to disregard it altogether as yet another uninformed expression of the same boring and somewhat stale pattern, even if somewhat out of joint with present times. Nevertheless, I think that it might not be out of place to say a few words here at a gathering that is devoted to discussing the American understanding of India.

The author, one James Gardner, apparently peeved by the fact that nowadays, and I quote him, "everybody seems to love India," goes on to review the Washington exhibition expatiating on what he calls the Indian's freakish aptitude for sculpture. In the process he makes many remarks that can only be characterized as unsubstantiated and foolish. To choose out a few random examples, there are references to "the rich and lascivious forms carved into the living rock at Mahabalipuram;" the Didarganj Yaksi as an application of the imported Persian style to a native motif; the compatibility of the "face of the Buddha with the chiseled modelling of the Venus of Milos;" and "the perfect roundness and protuberance of the Buddha's belly ... endowed [of all things] with thrilling energy." I can perhaps understand Mr. Gardner's views as a reaction to equally confused and uncritical hyperbole in the muddled and fanciful explanations and praises of Indian art that we now and then see. But what is surprising is that the editorial board of a reputed magazine would let pass as pertinent to any subject, let alone a less familiar one like Indian art, such a rush of subjective opinion in rather charged language. But to proceed. Having disposed of sculpture, Mr. Gardner gives a mercifully short account of Indian painting, which, with the exception of Ajanta, he characterizes as "essentially Arabic," whatever that may mean. After this display of how little he knows of what it is all about, he comes to the abrupt conclusion in the last two paragraphs that "our art," by which I suspect he must mean European art, is superior to Indian art. The reasons are fired off briefly and confidently, argument and logic being given even shorter shrift than usual. The Limbourg brothers and their contemporaries are superior, according to him, certainly in quality and probably quantity of production to the entire achievement of Rajput and what he calls Muslim miniature painting; similarly, all the architecture of India does not equal one century of French Gothic; and the "sculpture of India is honored by being spoken of as the equal of the sculpture of medieval France, and France," he assures us, "is only a small part of our Western civilization, and not necessarily the best."

All that one can say to someone who goes on like this is what Mr. Gardner himself proposes to say of a person who prefers Anton Mengs to Raphael: "he simply does not know what he is talking about." It is all so familiar, a *deja vu* not unlike James Fergusson, who even as he praised the high quality of Indian architecture and its adherence to truth, was never in doubt and did not hesitate to repeat that the Indians were incapable of profound thoughts and their expressions compared to the Anglo-Saxon.[19] Fergusson wrote, we may note, not in 1986 but in 1876, more than a hundred years ago. However much we may disagree with Fergusson, at least he had earned the right to say what he did because of the depth and acuity with which he studied the subject. Mr. Gardner shows no signs of either. I suppose that there will always be people like him, ready to write what comes into their fancy. We, too, are humbled by the knowledge that, paraphrasing J.R.R. Tolkien, though our eyes of flame may sometimes prove searchlights, their range is short.

DISCUSSION

In response to questions, Dr. Chandra explained Coomaraswamy's loss of zest for collecting by suggesting that he felt he was reaching beyond that stage to philosophy and metaphysics; but not mysticism: that suggestion would have offended him. He acquired his own collection largely in

Rajasthan and the Himalayas, but from dealers, not from their original owners.

As a part of the Festival, one collection of modern Indian art has come to America, and the Indo-U.S. Commission is planning to send an exhibit of modern American art to India. Up until now, little interchange has been achieved. Hardly any American museums have collections of modern Indian art.

He said George Birdwood's book, *Sva*, was one of the most sympathetic books on Indian village life, crafts and arts. It was generally conceded in Britain that Indian sculpture and higher arts demonstrated a very good sense of the decorative. But as soon as it came to idols, sculpture, imagery, richness, voluptuousness, it was just beyond them. When it came to Indian art, all that love that Birdwood had for India disappears.

A member of the audience found it curious that New England Puritanism hadn't prompted a response similar to that of the Victorian British evangelicals. The speaker noted that Coomaraswamy was himself a kind of Boston Brahmin. He and the leaders of Boston society shared a common intellectual interest and approach. They had the same concept of the role of original genius and believed that art is governed by strict and distinct rules. From the time he arrived in 1917 until things began to change in the 1930s, Coomaraswamy got along very well, and remained a Boston Brahmin to the end.

NOTES

1. See Arthur Christy, *The Orient in American Transcendentalism* (New York, 1963).
2. *Ideals of the East* (London, 1903), p. 24.
3. See her introduction in ibid., p. xii.
4. *Journal of the Royal Society of Arts* 58 (March 1910), p. 425.
5. *Rajput Painting* (Oxford, 1916).
6. For a clear statement of his views, see his *Theory of Painting* (Cambridge, Mass., 1912).
7. *Journal of the Indian Society of Oriental Art* 5 (1937), p.1.
8. *Catalogue of the Indian Collections in the Museum of Fine Arts, Boston*, 5 vols. (Boston, 1923-30); *History of Indian and Indonesian Art* (New York, 1927); *Yaksas*, 2 vols. (Washington, D.C., 1928-31); *Elements of Buddhist Iconography* (Cambridge, Mass., 1935); "Origin of the Buddha Image," *Art Bulletin* 9 (1927).
9. Ananda Coomaraswamy, "Reactions to Art in India," *Journal of the American Oriental Society* 52 (1932), pp. 213-20.

10. Eric Schroeder in S. Durai Raja Singham, *Homage to Coomaraswamy*, vol. 2 (1952), p. 78.
11. *Art Bulletin* 23 (1941), p. 173.
12. Quoted in Roger Lipsey, *Coomaraswamy, His Life and Work* (Princeton, N.J., 1977), p. 246.
13. Theodore Bowie, *Langdon Warner Through His Letters* (London, 1966), pp. 105-6.
14. W. Norman Brown, *The Story of Kalaka* (Washington, D.C., 1933) and *Miniature Paintings of the Jaina Kalpasutra* (Washington, D.C., 1934); Ludwig Bachhofer, *Early Indian Sculpture* (New York, 1929).
15. Cleveland Museum of Art, *Ancient Sculpture of India* (Cleveland, 1964); Stella Kramrisch, *Manifestations of Shiva* (Philadelphia, 1981).
16. Pramod Chandra, *The Sculpture of India, 3000 B.C.-1300 A.D.* (Cambridge, Mass., 1985); Stuart Cary Welch, *India* (New York, 1985); Stanislaw J. Czuma and Rekha Morris, *Kushan Sculpture: Images from Early India* (Cleveland, 1985).
17. Partha Mitter, *Much Maligned Monsters* (Oxford, 1977); Pramod Chandra, *On the Study of Indian Art* (Cambridge, Mass., 1983).
18. James Gardner, "Indian Art—and Ours," *Commentary* 81, no. 4 (April 1986), pp. 57-62.
19. Pramod Chandra, "The Study of Indian Temple Architecture," in Pramod Chandra, ed., *Studies in Indian Temple Architecture* (New Delhi, 1975).

American Understanding of India: A Historical Perspective

N. Gerald Barrier

America's contacts and resulting cultural interaction with India have occurred over two centuries. Many of the papers at this symposium deal with the intense academic involvement with India after the Second World War, and some of the audience and panelists have been active in South Asia for almost forty years. As several have noted, however, the roots of Indo-American encounters began long before the emergence of area studies and the burst of new government and educational programs in the 1960s. This essay reviews some of the earlier developments in an effort to put the encounters with India within a broader perspective. The interactions affected different Americans and segments of the public in various ways, diffusing a mixture of views and interpretations about India. The legacy, both in terms of institutional contacts and the resulting range of books and other printed matter that mark various stages of interactions and the experience of individuals and associations, nevertheless remains important in shaping how Americans interpret India.

From one perspective, much of American academic and intellectual encounter with India in the nineteenth century was molded or at least strongly influenced by European views. Europe had rediscovered India by the late 1700s, and a combination of mercantile, religious and scholarly interest in the subcontinent produced a substantial literature. Travelogues, histories, scholarly treatises in philology and the classics—an increasing number circulated in Europe and through reprint arrangements or library acquisition became readily available in the United States. Too, American scholars trained in European institutions and returned to establish centers of Indological and comparative research in institutions such as Yale and Harvard. American views of India went far beyond those captured in a European prism, however; Americans were interested and personally involved in the civilization of India in their own right. The fact that literally hundreds of titles on India were published by American firms prior to 1900 underscores American curiosity and interest in things Indian. That interest grew out of at least six strands or channels that linked America with British India. Economic, political and intellectual developments in the United States fostered more direct and vital links. As Americans created new institutions or modified those borrowed from Europe, they worked out their own relationships with and understanding of South Asia.

The first direct connection came from trade and concomitant consular activities. After 1784, American ships sailed regularly from Salem and Boston to Indian ports. Tea and coffee, along with cotton goods, came westward, and with the advent of the clipper ships, ice swiftly moved toward the east. These commercial enterprises produced intellectual curiosity, accounts of travel and trade and a gradual circulation of Indian literature. The connection with India was broadened and further institutionalized by the growth of American diplomatic institutions, first at Calcutta and then in other parts of India.

Trade and diplomacy had a far broader effect than just bringing a handful of Americans to India. The accompanying stories and information whetted the appetites of prospective adventurers and circulated information on India's religious and social life. With more background and better access to the subcontinent, individual travellers and those connected with organizations, such as missionaries, visited India and published articles and books on their experiences. Several hundred personal accounts were published between 1801 and 1930. Some reported on famine or art tours, while others, such as Mark Twain, wrote popular books on their Indian escapades. Following a three-month tour in 1896, Twain devoted 200 pages in *Following the Equator* to observations and a monologue on India. The book went through various editions and, despite inaccuracies and prejudice, helped stimulate new interest in another civilization.

Missionary activities brought Americans into greatest contact with India. From 1812 onward, American missions spread throughout India, until by 1900 approximately forty societies had missions or Christian-related institutions in India. Missionary activities and attitudes toward the civilization in which they worked varied across a broad spectrum. Some challenged other Americans to save the heathen people, while others focused on social programs and education. Over time, the American missionaries often became advocates for India and a few even endangered their work by openly championing Gandhi and the nationalist cause. They left behind a network of institutions and brought America very directly in contact with at least a part of India. Publishing over thirty journals, generating annual study guides on India (one small volume went through several reprints and reached over 200,000 in a study program), and lecturing in churches, schools and public halls, the U.S. missionaries promulgated both their faith and a vision of the milieu and culture to which they devoted a life's work.

The different organizations and approaches to missions were mirrored in the varied life-styles and ways that missionaries worked out an understanding of their faith. Some worked within formal channels, preaching, teaching or providing medical services. In south India, for example, the Scudders mixed medicine with preaching and at the same time wrote numerous tracts in the Telugu language. Others were more iconoclastic, such as Sadhu Hagenstein in the Central Provinces, who tried to communicate with Indians by setting up an ashram and adopting a life-style reminiscent of an Indian saint. Similarly, George Bowen in Bombay supported himself through journalism and, in addition to contributing to Marathi literature, circulated many books and tracts in the United States. Sam Higginbottom illustrated a new breed of missionary involved in economic issues and agricultural development. He organized the Allahabad Agricultural Institute and, advising both the British and, later, Nehru, helped lay the foundation for fresh approaches to rural education and development that became prominent after 1947.

Trade, curiosity and missions may have brought Americans to India, but at the same time Indian religious ideas and institutions were moving westward and reached Americans at home. During the last century, Hinduism, Buddhism and variations of those faiths gradually became part of American culture. Influence was incomplete and frequently limited to specific groups or areas, but the experience, as with other contacts, prepared the ground for improved communication between the two countries and at the same time produced a substantial literary record.

Even before the pivotal World Parliament of Religions in 1893, several links between American religious societies and India should be mentioned. One of the earliest and in some ways the most dynamic was the relationship between Unitarians and Hindu reformers in Bengal. William Adams introduced Rammohun Roy to Boston reformers and, sometime later, Unitarian missionary efforts reached Calcutta. Philip Ganguli, a convert, visited Boston in 1860 followed by tours of prominent Indians such as Protap Mazumdar in 1883. In addition to widening the American world-view and familiarizing many with current developments in India, the Unitarian efforts helped create a positive view of modern Indian religious movements and set the stage for political cooperation with Indian nationalists in later years.

Hinduism also had a short-lived but notable influence on American Transcendentalists. The intellectuals caught up with the idealism, romanticism and mysticism represented in the writings of Emerson and Thoreau felt somewhat comfortable with aspects of Indian metaphysics and practical dimensions of Indian daily life. Emerson wrote on *maya*, was intrigued by the notion of *karma* and knew quite a bit about the *Bhagavad Gita* in translation. Thoreau also tried to integrate Hindu ideas into his life and selected from Hindu scriptures those concepts that seemed relevant to his situation. His essays, in turn, later were to support some of Gandhi's notions about non-violence and serve as one of the intellectual bases for passive resistance among subsequent generations. Also noteworthy was the Indian influence on the nascent theosophical movement headed by Madame H.P. Blavatsky and Colonel Henry Steele Alcott. The internal struggles among the theosophists generated a massive literature and not a few public and legal explosions. One interesting outgrowth was the creation of a related Utopian community in Point Loma, California (*c.* 1897 to the late 1930s).

Growing involvement with non-Western religious traditions created the intellectual climate culminating in the World Parliament of Religions held in conjunction with the Columbia Exposition in Chicago in 1893. The Parliament was intended to relate humanism and religious values to technology, the primary focus of the Exposition. It brought to America several Indian leaders, but the most notable in the long run was a swami of the Ramakrishna order, Vivekananda. He toured the United States and began organizing Vedanta societies, each with its own separate identity and an imported religious leader sent to minister to the spiritual and educational needs of the membership. The centers in a dozen major cities constituted a nexus of informed interest in India and permanently linked Americans with a vital Hindu religious order.

Touring swamis were part of another development exposing America to India, the evolution of an Indian community in the U.S. Several thousand Indians came to America between the early 1900s and 1920, settling primarily in the California area. Others came for education and returned home, with a few remaining to teach or become involved in business. Harassed by neighbors who feared a "tide of turbans" or a "Hindu invasion," the immigrants lost many of their rights in the 1920s and further immigration was effectively blocked. Nevertheless, the small Indian population became active in the public life of their new country and, as excellent publicists, they formed associations that defended personal interests and at the same time sought to explain India to their fellow Americans.

Indians' efforts to mobilize public opinion involved both organizations and individual campaigns. In California, the Hindustan Ghadar (Mutiny) Party issued rousing calls for revolution and appealed for American help in throwing the imperialists out of their homeland. Because of pressure from the British and an ill-fated alliance between the group and the Germans in the First World War, the Ghadar Party became persecuted and generally failed to generate pro-Indian public opinion. Other Indians in New York were more successful in building support among American intellectuals and putting forth the case for India. Lajpat Rai and his organization, the Indian Home Rule League of America, for example, published a newspaper and issued numerous books and tracts with the aid of friends such as publisher Ben Huebsch. A few politicians (most notably William Lloyd Garrison and Robert LaFollette) gave assistance as did the editor of the *New Republic* and members of a new group, Friends of Freedom for India. The campaign to portray India in a positive light received a boost in 1913 when Rabindranath Tagore received the Nobel Prize for literature, toured the U.S. and arranged for many of his stories and books to be published by Macmillan.

Among the major interpreters of Indian civilization was Sudhindra Nath Bose, a teacher at the State University of Iowa, who lectured widely and wrote a stream of articles on the Indian experience in America. Bose also went head-to-head with several Congressmen in a 1914 hearing on the limitation of Indian immigrants. Using statistics and well-organized arguments, Bose countered racist charges about Indian morals, cleanliness and illiteracy and also used Western scholarship to convince the committee that Indians were of Aryan stock. Another important interpreter of Indian culture was Dhan Gopal Mukerji, who wrote novels, children's stories and personal accounts of life in India and America. The most energetic publicist, however, was Dr. Haridas T. Muzumdar, who studied at Columbia, Chicago and Wisconsin, and published books on India, Gandhi and public affairs.

Indians and their allies confronted a major attack on Indian society and religion in 1927 when Katherine Mayo issued *Mother India*. Labeled a "drain inspector's report" by Gandhi, the book evoked a strong reaction in America. The press response was mixed but many editorials and public pronouncements supported India and questioned the validity of Mayo's claims.

The issues raised by Mayo's volume were met in part by a new set of allies for India, a small but growing network of American academics with training in the study of Indian civilization, languages and literatures. Some early research and writing on Indian literature and language came from isolated scholars such as Albert Pike of Little Rock, who made a translation of the *Rig Veda*. The more common pattern, however, was for scholars to group together in organizations or to affiliate with major universities. Founded in 1842, the American Oriental Society generated substantial scholarly research and publication on India, particularly in the area of comparative philology. The great Sanskritists of the period, such as E.E. Salisbury, W.D. Whitten, Charles Rockwell Lanman and their successors, helped lead the AOS and made the study of Indian classical language and literature an important part of the curriculum of Harvard and Yale. Other Harvard scholars, such as Josiah Royce, Henry Clark Warren and James Haughton Woods studied Indian religion and incorporated Indian ideas in their own study and teaching.

Undoubtedly the most important interpreter of Indian tradition was not an American but rather the keeper of Indian art at the Boston Museum of Fine Arts, Ananda K. Coomaraswamy. As Professor Pramod Chandra's essay suggests, Coomaraswamy's contributions included many scholarly works, lectures and a general stimulation of discussion about Indian matters.

An assortment of scholars joined Coomaraswamy and others to broaden and enrich understanding between America and India. One measure of their success was the creation of Sanskrit departments and the spread of study of Indic literature and philosophy at a dozen universities. Also in abundance were more manuscripts, documents and printed books on scholarly subjects. Two ACLS-sponsored surveys of printed Indological texts, translations and manuscripts (1933, 1938) underscored the richness of U.S. holdings, complemented by the art and archaeological collections of several public and university museums.

By the late 1920s, Americans thus had been exposed to a range of perspectives on India, from popular accounts and missionary reports to publications and lectures by those studying religion, philosophy and literature. The strands and channels of information intertwined. Itinerant swamis lectured to philosophy departments and learned Sanskritists talked to missionary societies or at civic luncheons. Specialists in comparative religion trained mission workers while at the same time developing a scholarly tradition in the study of Indian religious thought.

During the next two decades, the patterns persisted with a notable expansion of contacts between the public and India. Tourists travelled more frequently and new generations of academics appeared led by professors such as Franklin Edgerton and later W. Norman Brown. The series of East-West philosophers' conferences, which began in 1939, also facilitated dialogue between Indian and American specialists. American involvement with India nevertheless took a new turn after the 1920s. The first sign of the shift began with the rise of Gandhi in Indian politics and the spectacle of a non-violent war against imperialism, a dramatic struggle that captured the attention of America and helped reinforce positive attitudes toward Indian society and values. Imperial struggle became joined with world conflict in 1941 as India increasingly became identified with the Allied war effort and the survival of the West. The war further involved Americans in a civilization and region now judged vital to U.S. interests.

As several scholarly works have shown, interest in Gandhi and images of his life and message fluctuated widely in response to events in India and perceptions of American self-interest. Portrayed as a hero or villain (the latter often a perspective encouraged by British propagandists operating in the United States), Gandhi stirred emotions and found many American allies. Indian nationalism also attracted much attention, with Americans sometimes drawing parallels between their own revolution and the effort of Indians to overthrow a colonial power. The Salt March in 1930 stunned America, as did British efforts to censor American reporters and prevent news coverage of attacks on unarmed Indians. Besides Gandhi being featured as *Time*'s man of the year in January 1931, the Indian struggle brought more reporters and observers to the subcontinent and accelerated the circulation of information, not only on politics but other aspects of Indian daily life. Gandhi's subsequent decision to force the British to "quit India" at the outset of the War brought a backlash accompanied by a concerted propaganda campaign by the nationalists and the British. New pro-Indian publicists joined the fray, such as Dr. Anup Singh, who cooperated with the John Day Publishing Company in printing a series of books on India including works by Nehru and Gandhi. Krishnalal Shridharani used his degrees in sociology and journalism from Columbia to build a substantial network among American intellectuals. The king of the propagandists and a master lobbyist, Jagjit Singh, ran a journal and worked effectively to incorporate leading American journalists, such as Drew Pearson, in the struggle for Indian independence. He almost singlehandedly put together a Congressional coalition that championed the 1946 Immigration Act, notable both for reopening America to Indian immigrants as well as restoring citizenship to those who had been unfairly stripped of their rights earlier. These and other Indians found allies among journalists and prominent authors. John Gunther and Pearl Buck called for a free India, and the newest and most prolific convert, Louis Fischer, visited Gandhi and championed India.

The War and its aftermath signalled the approach of a new era in Indo-

American relations. Thousands of American troops experienced India first-hand, as did newsmen who remained knowledgeable commentators on events there. Too, the war stimulated study of India and brought individuals and organizations into closer contact through efforts to understand, document and help with the challenges of India's nascent independence. Out of the ashes of war, partition and Gandhi's death emerged a new Indian nation. New channels linked India and America. Popular culture and religious belief in the United States underwent change, affected partly by the spread of Hindu or other religious organizations from India. More Americans visited India and helped demolish images and barriers. Direct contact was also facilitated by the rapid growth of the Indian community in the United States after the liberalization of immigration laws in 1965. The new Americans continued to interpret their culture and became a visible model for cultural understanding. Indian literature, films and the performing arts became more accepted elements of American life. As Daniel Neuman has demonstrated, for example, the teaching and performance of Indian music has spread across America well beyond the bounds of academic institutions. In addition, Indian religious and sectarian movements intensified this rediscovery of India. The elder Vedanta societies were joined by the followers of Swami Yogananda, a variety of yoga schools and groups, Meher Baba centers and the devotional message of the International Society for Krishna Consciousness. Other movements underwent significant change in America, such as the 3HO organization that evolved from yogic practices to an incorporation of Sikh symbols and traditions.

Like the roots of the Banyan tree, the century-old interest in things Indian has reached down into the soil of American culture and reappeared again and again, sometimes in unexpected ways or forms. Although American museums and individual collectors did not begin serious acquisition of Indian artifacts and art objects until recently, the collections of Indian art in American institutions now rate among the best in the world. Indian views of life and reality also have stimulated new ways of thinking. Notions of *karma* and *dharma* frequently appear in post-War literature, while Hindu philosophy and related themes have become part of a sub-culture involving mysticism and the exploration of the limits of experience and knowing. Although the presentation of India in educational curricula still leaves much to be desired, more attempts have been made to integrate an understanding of Indian life and world-view into either special courses or social science offerings. Gandhian thought and Indian views on non-violence are regular elements in America's intellectual and political culture.

Martin Luther King Jr. turned to Gandhi's life and teachings for solace and direction, and America's involvement with non-violence and passive resistance, which neither began nor ended with the great civil rights leader, continues to make *satyagraha* a key value in protests over war, nuclear power or discrimination.

As Gandhian values are integrated into child-rearing, conflict resolution and community development, the original sources sometimes get lost or obscured, but the effect remains. The diffusion of Indian culture into American life has been incomplete and had mixed results, the product of a period of changing interests of individuals and segments of society.

A fresh and different kind of contact with India grew up after 1947, interactions fundamentally affecting Indo-American relations and our understanding of India. These revolved around the programs of the U.S. Government and its agencies, complemented and sometimes overshadowed by the work of foundations such as Ford and Rockefeller. Legacies include U.S. contributions to Indian agriculture, economics and education as well as the evolution of a new group of specialists committed to partnership with Indian colleagues. Joining these programs was a new type of academic involvement in India's past and present. Not limited as in the past to Indology and classical concerns, the new India specialists focussed on the social sciences, the humanities and systematic scholarly understanding. The new interpreters of India produced an impressive literature that continues to grow and enrich both civilizations.

India faced appreciable difficulties in the post-1947 era. Stabilizing relations with Pakistan and the warring super-powers was a formidable task, compounded by the domestic challenges such as drafting a constitution, bringing Indians together with a sense of national unity and dealing with domestic issues. Specialists from abroad pitched in to help. American advisers included Gardner Murphy, who worked with Indian colleagues to try and evaluate social tensions, Albert Mayer, a city planner and architect giving leadership for development and the Etawah Project and Alice and Daniel Thorner, who left America during the McCarthy period and worked on India's statistical and economic projects. The most substantive aid, however, came from American agencies and foundations.

Just as official U.S. policy toward India prior to 1947 had been determined largely in response to British imperial needs and pressures (particularly during the War), so in later years American fiscal and technical assistance were colored by fluctuating Indo-American relations, which at times resembled a roller coaster. Periods of close ties, particularly during the ambassadorships of Chester Bowles and John Galbraith, were followed quickly by estrangement, name-calling and hostility. A small wheat-loan program begun in 1951 was followed by extensive supply of food and aid under the provisions of the Agricultural Trade Development and Assistance Act (Public Law 480 of 1954). By 1971, America had provided almost ten billion dollars in the form of loans, technical assistance and a variety of grants. At the same time, thousands of Americans participated in joint ventures and assistance programs. In education, the U.S. Educational Foundation encouraged the exchange of scholars and teachers. The Peace Corps, begun in 1965 with approximately 600 volunteers and doubling that until its withdrawal in 1974, helped initiate many programs and, in the process, changed the lives and perspectives of innumerable Americans and their families at home. The USAID contracts linked American and Indian universities, with transfer of faculty, students and technology in a regular fashion. At the University of Missouri, Columbia, for example, over sixty faculty members spent time in India ranging from a year to eight years.

American foundations also joined Indian agencies and leaders in planning and development. The Rockefeller Foundation helped finance a range of projects on crop research and production and supported key institutions such as the Indian Agricultural Research Institute, the Indian Statistical Institute and the India International Center in New Delhi. From the early 1950s onward, the Ford Foundation made India the focus of a very expensive and broad-based program of development and research. With Douglas Ensminger at the helm, the Foundation developed close working relationships with key officials and in a spirit of cooperation assisted with major policy formulation in the 1950s and 1960s. As George Rosen's excellent book, *Western Economists and Eastern Societies* clearly demonstrates, the Foundation made a lasting impact on India while at the same time offering the opportunity for many young American specialists to combine theory and field experience. The Ford-supported MIT International Studies Center, for example, became a focus for basic research and policy discussions relating to Indian development.

The Ford Foundation's support for the MIT Center suggests another dimension of its evolving concerns, the attempt to support academic enterprises and the concomitant development of technical and area-study expertise in America. The pivotal international conference on Indian urbanization held at Berkeley in the summer of 1960, for example, received considerable Ford help. The Foundation committed increasing resources to area centers, and by 1971 had invested almost two hundred million dollars in international studies.

The handful of colleges and universities amassing South Asia resources did so in terms of existing institutional priorities. Cornell, for instance, had Ford funds to teach in the social sciences and agriculture. Penn's program, headed by Norman Brown, continued to build on a base of Indological studies, while Chicago's curriculum evolved from the interest of Robert Redfield in Great Traditions and Little Traditions. Chicago also developed an integrated Indian civilization course, received funds from Carnegie for internships and library acquisitions and both recruited and trained new generations of South Asianists with more depth in the social sciences and humanities. At Berkeley, Richard Park secured Ford funds for a "Modern India Project" funded between 1954 and 1957. The resulting research and publication included the *Indian Press Digest* and books and bibliographies that helped expand the young field of South Asian studies.

As discussed in this symposium, the Soviet launching of Sputnik in 1957 set the stage for a dramatic growth of federal funding for foreign language and area studies. The rest of the story is well known, with the expansion of the Association for Asian Studies, the creation of the American Institute of Indian Studies in 1961 and the evolution of a South Asia Regional Council and Committee on South Asia Libraries and Documentation.

The result? American academics are major interpreters of Indian tradition. Although the decline in federal and foundation support has continued since the early 1970s, Indian studies have been routinized and accepted as part of the curriculum not only in the universities with large centers such as Berkeley, Chicago, Penn, Columbia and Wisconsin, but now can be found in educational institutions across the country. Over three hundred colleges and universities offer one or more courses on India, often with several specialists teaching both general and discipline-oriented subjects relating to South Asia. This teaching, combined with the extensive American publication record, has expanded the knowledge about India throughout a large part of the American population. In the 1960s, Alan Watts could comment harshly on the chasm between popular interest in India and the work of the "dreary pandits" as represented by the earlier Indological research of the American Oriental Society: "The in-group of academic orientalists who, as librarians, philological nitpickers and scholarly drudges dissolve all creative interest into acidulated pedantry."[1] That certainly is not true today. Although area-trained South Asianists have no monopoly on understanding and interpreting India, they increasingly are involved in public forums, local secondary education and outreach.

The Festival of India has highlighted the vast pools of information and resources available in this country and at the same time offered a forum in which diverse groups and organizations can make their own contributions to cultural understanding. And yet, as this brief essay suggests, it would be a mistake to view the Festival as affording a one-time opportunity for Americans to encounter India. The Chairman of the Indian Advisory Committee for the Festival put the issue quite simply: "The Festival of India will provide to the people of the United States a new and, we hope, rewarding discovery. When the Festival ends, as all festivals must, will India leave behind a footprint?"[2] The query, of course, is rhetorical, but a satisfactory answer must address the meaning of the celebration. The Festival is just that, a culmination of interests and interactions at many levels, a renewal of experience and an opportunity for Indians and Americans alike to enjoy a living tradition already part of American public life.

This symposium gave me an opportunity to contemplate our corporate past, to try and fit together pieces of a puzzle as to where South Asian studies came from, its current state and its future role. During that experience and while preparing a final draft of my book on American publishing on India, I constantly was reminded about things Indian about me. Christopher Isherwood, a major interpreter of the Vedantic tradition, died in California, and a controversial guru closed his ashram and left America forever. My friend, Doug Ensminger, returned from yet another triumphal Indian trip where he renewed old acquaintances and undoubtedly laid the groundwork for fresh projects. Letters arrived, one from Haridas Muzumdar in Little Rock, another from Sikh friends requesting my participation in a summer youth camp. PBS's "All Things Considered" reviewed Indian films and a book on Muslims and the Partition. Public television also ran a well-researched documentary on Rajiv Gandhi and India's prospects for the future. I received two journals: the first, the latest number of *Hinduism Today*, surveyed the academic study of Hinduism in America, and shortly thereafter there came the Chicago *Outreach Bulletin* that praised the sectarian journal as an important vehicle for understanding currents in the Hindu religion. Martin Luther King Jr.'s life was celebrated for the first time as a national holiday. The review of a traumatic yet triumphal period in our own history again brought Gandhi and non-violence to the forefront; a local editor referred to King as America's Gandhi. Students from my Gandhi class helped lead the anti-apartheid, divestment movement on campus and talked freely about the relationship between ideology and action as they constructed a shanty town. Two days of discussing academic and public matters at this conference floods me with memories and new perspectives. I had the privilege of meeting old India hands, such as Jean Joyce and Marion Massen from the early days of the Ford Foundation, and the author of a seminal work on Indian civilization, M.N. Srinivas, who influenced my earliest work on India.

These and many experiences and perspectives reflected in this symposium point to the place of India in the American experience. There also lies the response to Pupul Jayakar's question. The Festival of India leaves behind memories, encounters, catalogs and yet another bookshelf of monumental publications. Yes, the footprints remain but, more importantly, the popular and scholarly appreciation of India already has deep roots in American soil and, like the Banyan tree, will appear again and again, bearing fruit and enriching our lives.

DISCUSSION

Dr. Rudolph commented that there is a kind of systematic negative theme forming part of the history of the American sense of India that has certain common qualities from Katherine Mayo through Arthur Koestler to the article Pramod Chandra quoted. It reflects a nervous monotheistic unease with Indian society and philosophy. This is less visible from the perspective of the 1960s, which adopted a kind of polytheistic spirit that was receptive to the Indian experience. Dr. Barrier said that Mayo was offensive to some British authorities, and her volume of photographs was banned. Dr. Chandra remarked that the American Charles Eliot Norton, who arrived in India in 1846 aboard a trading ship stocked with hides, was outspoken in his criticism of the British for the terrible condition of the Indians he observed. Norton judged that the Indians had not reached their potential because the British had done everything they could to prevent it. Dr. White pointed out that there were two or three Americans who became nuns and monks of the Ramakrishna Mission, one of whom was a naturalized Dutchman who had achieved eminence in the order when he died in India about the age of ninety. And in Myrtle Beach, South Carolina, noted Dr. Barrier, there is a Mir Baba Center which was established in the 1930s and still issues a newsletter. This is one of dozens if not hundreds of such organizations scattered across the United States publishing five or ten tracts a year and maybe a newsletter, none of which ever find their ways into public bibliographic records. He said that his guide, cited below, tried to identify these publications. Lakshmi Crane added that between 1750 and 1770, three American artists from Philadelphia are said to have followed Johann Zoffany to India. Although merchants from Philadelphia paid their fares, they painted for British patrons and their paintings ended up in Britain. A question was asked about Agnes Smedley, whose India career has received little attention, and whose reputation in India, particularly in Bengal, was negative. She was an avid propagandist for India as well as a birth-control advocate. But references to her are few.

Professor Harold Gould commented on the skills of Jagjit Singh, who played a very important role in lobbying Congress on behalf of Indian immigration, in which he secured the support, surprisingly, of conservative Representative Karl Mundt, and to get India placed on the list of potential recipients of UNRRA relief during the 1946 Bengal famine, in which he was opposed by no less a figure than Dean Acheson. Dr. Barrier noted that a lot of famine victims died before the U.S. took any action.

NOTES

* This paper is based on research made possible by grants from the Research Council, University of Missouri, Columbia, and the Ford Foundation.

1. Alan Watts, *In My Own: An Autobiography, 1915-1965* (1972), p.143.
2. *Festival of India in the United States, 1985-1986* (1985), p.10.

APPENDIX
SOURCES ON THE AMERICAN-INDIAN ENCOUNTER

A more detailed treatment of the historical interaction between America and India, along with a review of relevant documents and secondary materials can be found in N. Gerald Barrier, *India and America: American Publishing on India, 1930-1985* (Manohar, AIIS, 1986). Another comprehensive survey of bibliographical sources is Maureen Patterson's *South Asian Civilization: A Bibliographic Synthesis* (Chicago, 1981). The Missionary Research Library *Catalog*, 17 vols. (1968) and the *Catalog* of the Ames Library of South Asia, University of Minnesota, 16 vols. (1980) contain references to much of the nineteenth century literature. Also useful as general guides to issues are W. Norman Brown, *The United States and India and Pakistan* (Harvard, various edns., 1953-72) and Norman D. Palmer, *The United States and India* (Praeger, 1984)

Several academic studies trace the varied dimensions of America's encounters with India during the nineteenth century. Orientalism and European intellectual developments are discussed in Edward W. Said, *Orientalism* (Pantheon, 1978) and Raymond Schwab, *The Oriental Renaissance* (Columbia, 1984). Diplomacy and trade are reviewed in G. Bhagat, *Americans in India* (1970). India's cultural influence has been the focus of three monographs: Arthur Christy, *The Orient in American Transcendentalism* (Columbia, 1932; repr.); Dale Riepe, *The Philosophy of India and its Impact on American Thought* (Charles C. Thomas, 1970); and Carl T. Jackson, *The Oriental Religions and American Thought* (Greenwood, 1981). Missionary activities receive attention in an un-published dissertation by Earl Schmidt, "American Relations with South Asia, 1900-1940" (Pennsylvania, 1955). Spencer Lavan's *Unitarians and India*, 2nd edn. (Beacon, 1984) provides a provocative treatment of a little-known phase of American cultural interaction with India, while background on the Theosophist movement and Ramakrishna can be found in J. Stillson Judah, *The History and Philosophy of the Metaphysical Movements in America* (Westminster, 1967); Harold W. French, *The Swan's Wide Waters: Ramakrishna and Western Culture* (Kennikat, 1974); and Wendell M. Thomas, *Hinduism Invades America* (Beacon, 1930).

The South Asia Center, University of California, Berkeley, soon will publish a guide to the literature on and by Indians residing in the United States. Useful secondary sources include Gary R. Hess, "The Forgotten Asian Americans: The East India Community in the United States," in Norris Hundley, ed., *The Asian American* (Clio, 1978); essays in S. Chandrasekhar, ed., *From India to America* (Population Review, 1982); and H. Brett Melendy, *Asians in America* (Twayne, 1977: esp. pp.173-245). Background on Indians and American politics includes an unpublished dissertation by N.G. Rathore, "Indian Agitation in the U.S." (Columbia, 1965); Gary Hess, *America Encounters India* (Johns Hopkins Press, 1971); and a series of monographs by M.S. Venkataramani. A useful analysis and collection of documents on Gandhi's impact is Charles Chatfield, ed., *The Americanization of Gandhi: Images of the Mahatma* (Garland, 1976).

In the post-1947 period, Robert McDermott's introduction to issues and the literature of Indian sects and their influence in America, "Indian Spirituality in the West: a Bibliographical Mapping," *Philosophy East and West*, vol. 25, pp. 213-39, remains a standard work. Further information on the movements and their literature can be found in Barrier, *India and America*, as well as in monographs by Charles White, Jacob Needleman, Francine Daner, Stillson Judah, Harold French, Robert Elwood and Marvin Harper. On the early phase of India's development program and foreign assistance, see Carl Taylor, Douglas Ensminger, Helen Johnson and Jean Joyce, *India's Roots of Democracy* (Orient Longmans, 1965). George Rosen has written a definitive study on the MIT program and the Ford Foundation in India, *Western Economists and Eastern Societies: Agents of Change in South Asia, 1950-1970* (Johns Hopkins, 1985). The history of one South Asia program and the evolution of the field as a whole is found in Richard H. Davis, *South Asia at Chicago: A History* (Chicago, 1985), while overall assessments of major events and programmatic changes are given in Richard D. Lambert, *Resources for South Asian Studies in the United States* (Pennsylvania, 1962); and Lambert, *Beyond Growth* (Association of American Universities, 1984).

Many of the issues and references to the literature surrounding the current state of Indian studies in America are contained in other symposium papers. The American Institute of Indian Studies has published numerous collections of American scholarship on India including Joanna Williams, ed., *Kaladarshana: American Studies in the Art of India* (1981); Sylvia Vatuk, ed., *American Studies in the Anthropology of India* (1978); Gregory Possehl, ed., *Harappan Civilization* (1984); and Frederick Asher, ed., *Indian Epigraphy* (1985). In addition to the many collections of papers resulting from Festival of India seminars and several beautiful catalogs of exhibits, a useful overview of activities and the general scope of the celebration is in *Festival of India in the United States, 1985-1986* (Abrams, 1985).

An Ethnography of the American Experience of Indian Music

Daniel M. Neuman

Indian music is perhaps the most widely distributed artifact of Indian culture in the United States. Accordingly, along with Air India's Maharaja, beautiful women in *saris* and distinguished, albeit vaguely threatening, men in turbans, musical instruments such as the *sitar*, *vina* and *tabla* as well as the sounds they make are among the most recognized of Indian icons in the United States.

An important element in the ongoing development of conceptions about India is the presence of courses and programs on Indian music throughout the United States and Canada. This seemingly strictly academic phenomenon interfaces widely with a more general public, a point to which I shall return below. The scholarly research on and the teaching of Indian musical culture ought to be thoroughly documented even though it is just recent history. Here I present only the broadest outline of such a history.

Indian Music in the Academy

It is often a surprise to the uninitiated to learn about the extensive offerings of courses on Indian music in North American universities taught by what are now three generations of scholars, the earliest of whom conducted their research in the mid-1950s.

There are perhaps two ways of discussing American (by which I mean both Canadian and United States) scholarship on Indian music. One is from the perspective of institutions. This is not unlike how one might characterize contributions of individual artists or their stylistic schools in India.

The first two individuals to be discussed are Robert Brown, currently at San Diego State University, and Harold Powers, currently at Princeton University. Brown went from UCLA to develop the first major program in Indian music in the United States at Wesleyan University, a legacy still continued through the person of T. Visvanathan. Both Brown and Powers conducted fieldwork in India in the middle 1950s and completed their dissertations somewhat later (1959 for Powers and 1965 for Brown). Neither dissertation is published, but both have been widely cited through the years.

There are two other scholars who had an interest and did work in India but whose role is somewhat different. Nazir Jairazbhoy is the same generation as Powers and Brown but his influence in North America was not decisive until he published his seminal work in 1971[1] and moved soon thereafter to UCLA. The other person is Robert Garfias, who is not known as an Indian musical scholar, but who was responsible for inviting musicians to this country as well as recording them very early on. He had good relationships with Balasaraswati, Ravi Shankar, Ali Akbar Khan, Zia M. Dagar and a host of other Indian artists.

Although I don't know when the first courses on Indian music were offered in the United States, I do know that by the 1960s there were visiting artists from India and courses taught on a regular basis at UCLA, Wesleyan University, the University of Illinois and the University of Washington.

Wesleyan, however, occupies a special place in this history since it was the first program in which a major and sustained Indian musical presence was established. Through a remarkable coincidence of good luck (a large endowment that enabled the Center for World Music to be built), Robert Brown's energy and vision, which attracted a very large number of students both as performers and as scholars of Indian music, and his ability in most cases to invite the right artists, Wesleyan became a seat of Indian music in North America. In the late 1960s there were at least four Indian musicians resident at one time there, two from north India and two from the south. One of the latter is T. Vishvanathan, who is still an artist in residence at Wesleyan, as was his brother, the late and very much lamented Tagore Ranganathan. Bob Becker, David Reck and, of course, the late Jon Higgins were among the significant products of Wesleyan.

Robert Brown and T. Vishvanathan were the teachers of the late Jon Higgins, who himself became a celebrated performer in India[2] and a scholar and teacher at York University in Canada and somewhat later at Wesleyan, where he had earlier been a student. After his untimely death, Higgins' influence as performer, scholar and teacher has been publicly recognized by a memorial scholarship established in his name by the Canadian Indian music organization, Ragamala.[3]

The other important center was UCLA, which had visiting artists such as T. Visvanathan and afterwards Gayatri Kassebaum, nee Rajapur.[4] Although UCLA produced notable Indianists, such as Robert Brown and later Bonnie Wade, it was not until Nazir Jairazbhoy joined the faculty that UCLA had its own Indian scholar. One of Jairazbhoy's first students from UCLA was Peter Manuel, who is currently teaching at Columbia University.

The University of Hawaii, although only offering the Master's degree in ethnomusicology, has had an inordinately large influence in Indian musical scholarship in the United States. Ranganaiki Ayyangar, Gayatri Kassebaum, Rebecca Stewart nee Adriaanz and Ted Solis have made important contributions to the field, and in some cases continue to do so. Ranganaiki (who received her Ph.D. under Powers) is now head of the music department at Banaras Hindu University, the most important university department of music in India. Stewart's unpublished dissertation on the *tabla*[5] has had significant influence in the field, and is in my opinion still the most important source in English on north Indian drumming traditions. And although Ted Solis worked on a different area for his Ph.D., his Master's thesis on the *sarod* is widely respected by those who know it.

The University of Illinois has also had visiting professors such as S.B. Ramanathan (1965-66), Ranganaiki Ayyangar and Nazir Jairazbhoy as well as an active interest in south Indian music on the part of Bruno Nettl, who conducted fieldwork there several years ago. Charles Capwell, who has worked on Bengali musical traditions, has been on the faculty at Illinois since the early 1980s. Daniel Neuman and Steven Slawek were trained there.

At the University of Washington, visiting artists from India have been an active part of the program since its founding by Robert Garfias in the early 1960s. Artists such as Z.M. Dagar, Sabri Khan, Yunus Khan, Sharmista Sen, to name recent north Indian visitors, have spent at least a full academic year in residence. Until recently, the University of Washington had a faculty composed entirely of individuals who had conducted fieldwork in India: Ter Ellingson, who is a Tibetan specialist, Lorraine Sakata, who is an Afghan specialist but has worked in Rajasthan and Daniel Neuman, who is an India specialist.

U.C. Berkeley has had a program in ethnomusicology since 1975 when Bonnie Wade joined the faculty. Professor Wade has a number of students working on India and has had visitors such as Komal Kothari of Rupayanstan Institute in Rajasthan as well as various performing artists.

Mention must also be made of the sole music conservatory of Indian music in the United States, the Ali Akbar College of Music in San Raphael, California, which has succeeded in training fine performers of Indian music many of whom have continued their study in India.

Other universities which have programs or courses involving the music of India include the following with their associated faculty: The University of Texas, Steve Slawek; Amherst College, David Reck; New England Conservatory of Music, Peter Row; Colgate University, William Skelton; San Diego State University, Robert Brown; York University, L. Shankar; and the University of Alberta, Regula Qureshi.

Academic Research

An overview of some of the important research conducted on the music of India during the last three decades can only be suggestive in the absence of a more comprehensive treatment.

Harold Powers, first at the University of Pennsylvania and now Princeton University, has had a very important influence on American research on Indian music. His major contributions have covered many areas, particularly the comparative study of Hindustani and Karnatak *raga*s. His monograph-sized article in Grove's *Encyclopedia of Music and Musicians* provides the most comprehensive and reliable overview of classical Indian music available in English. It is magisterial in scope and authority. It is what I recommend if one is going to read a single work on Indian music. Powers has influenced many scholars and has had a number of students, although only Ranganaiki Ayyangar finished a degree under him in the field of Indian music.

Equally important have been the publications of Nazir Jairazbhoy, whose theoretical work on the north Indian *raga*s published in 1971 was considered by some to have been the most important publication in ethnomusicology in the previous decade. His students include Peter Manuel, who has worked on *thumri* (and is an excellent sitarist as well), and Gordon Thomson, who has worked on folk musicians in Gujarat.

Bob Brown's dissertation on the *mridangam*[6] and a short article on Indian music for the University of Wisconsin syllabus on South Asia[7] have both been influential. This last is the best short summary on Indian music. His impact is more important for his institutional contributions than any body of scholarship, although he is currently engaged with Smithsonian-sponsored research on rhythm systems in India.

Professor Bonnie Wade has written or edited several books, two of which deal exclusively with India. The first was a textbook on north and south Indian music widely used in classes on the subject. Her most recent book on *khyal* and *gharana* styles promises to be a landmark study on the relationship between musical style and social organization in north Indian vocal traditions.[8]

Regula Qureshi, an anthropologist trained at Alberta who is an accomplished cellist and *sarangi* (Indian fiddle) player, has been working on the music of Pakistan and India for several years now. She has published extensively on the music of Pakistan and India, particularly the music of the Sufi traditions. Her recent book on *qawwali* will make an impact on performance studies since her work involves new methodological uses of videotape and analysis.[9]

Charles Capwell has recently published a book on the musical traditions of the Bauls of Bengal.[10] This is the first of a number of monographs expected during the next few years on music of India's non-classical traditions.

Joan Erdman, an anthropologist trained at the University of Chicago, has worked on the archives of the royal household of Jaipur and has gathered valuable archival material on the role of court-employed musicians in Jaipur. Her book on patronage in Rajasthan was recently published in India.[11] She has also published on Indian dance and has conducted extensive research on the renowned Indian dancer, Uday Shankar.

Most recently, a book about *sitar* performance practice has been published by Steve Slawek. Since it was published in India, it may take some time to have an impact here, but it looks to be an important contribution, in part because Ravi Shankar himself thinks especially highly of Slawek's knowledge and exceptional capabilities as a performer.[12]

Other important research which unfortunately has not yet found its way into monograph-length publication has been done by Edward Henry (San Diego State University) on village music in eastern U.P., Jennifer Post (Middlebury College) on women's music in western India, and T. Vishvanathan on *alpana* performance practice in the Karnatak tradition. To this list must be added the dissertations mentioned earlier of both Harold Powers and Bob Brown, both widely cited but never published works.

This, of course, only scratches the surface of the very extensive research conducted on Indian music in recent decades. One other phenomenon that has had a significant impact just since 1981 has been the establishment of the Archive and Research Centre for Ethnomusicology in Delhi, India.

The Archive and Research Centre was an idea developed by Nazir Jairazbhoy, who is its founder. Since much research had been conducted in India with many recordings being made, Jairazbhoy felt strongly that facilities should be made available to ensure that collections or copies of them were kept in India and that research facilities be made available in India to scholars working on the performing arts of India. Originally funded by the Ford Foundation and the Smithsonian Institution working through the American Institute of Indian Studies, the Archive and Research Centre for Ethnomusicology (ARCE) is an American organization located in India and serving as a research center for all scholars of Indian music. In addition to serving as an archive for a rapidly growing collection, the ARCE has also sponsored two international seminars, one on documentation and the other on the relationship between music and texts.

Non-Academic Musical Phenomena

Since the early 1950s (and actually even earlier through dance), Indian music has become an increasingly common public phenomenon in the United States. For example, film scores such as Ravi Shankar's score for the film *Charley*, or Vilayat Khan's for *Guru* have familiarized audiences with the sound of the *sitar* and *tabla*, also now common on commercial soundtracks for everything from television commercials to popular and jazz recordings.

Aside from Ravi Shankar and Ali Akbar Khan concerts, many of which have been released as live and studio recordings, a younger generation of Indian musicians such as Zakir Hussein, L. Shankar and L. Subramaniam have made a major musical impact in the United States through their concerts and recordings of fusion music (often coupled with traditional classical performances), with the result that aspects of Indian musical ideas have been very widely disseminated to all kinds of audiences in the United States.

Carnegie Hall recitals for Indian performers have created an enhanced forum and a context of credibility for Indian classical music and even non-classical forms. During the Festival of India in 1985-86, for example, non-classical musicians were heard throughout the United States as they toured under the auspices of the Festival.

Conversely, musical phenomena such as the concertos for *sitar* and orchestra composed by Ravi Shankar have introduced Western classical music listeners to at least some of the sounds of Indian music, if not its forms *per se*.

Indian music, including devotional, regional and popular film music as well as classical, has been broadcast in North America on an increasingly wide scale. Aside from programs targeted to Indians living in urban areas of North America, I know of Indian music programs that have been broadcast on a regular basis from places as divergent as Cambridge, Boulder and Seattle.

Although there is no formal study available on the impact that Indian music has had on American perceptions of India, there is no doubt that a significant factor in the formation of American perceptions of India has been the images, sounds and personalities of India's performing artists, a phenomenon that will almost certainly become more widespread in the future.[13]

Conclusion

Because of the coalescence of three phenomena during the 1960s—the popular and scholarly interest in Indian music, and the immigration of a relatively large number of middle-class Indians to the United States—there has emerged an interesting coalition of interest in continuing support for live Indian musical concerts. In virtually every major city in the United States as well as numerous smaller urban centers, live performances of Indian music can be expected to be heard at least sometime during a year. Performances are provided not only by touring professional musicians but also by a large and active amateur performing tradition imported from India and, if anything, even more viable in the United States.

The sound and the structures of Indian musical performance genres will continue to be heard by a larger as well as more heterogeneous audience in the United States. And, if through the hearing there continues to evolve a level of listening, Indian music will provide an increasingly enlarged and more subtly informed perception of India itself.

DISCUSSION

Dr. Hart commented on the apparently increasing interest on the part of Indian communities living in the United States in having daughters study *Bharata Natyam* with local teachers and in sponsoring large festival dance performances. Dr. Robins-Mowry wondered if musical and dance forms tend to become altered in the process of being reproduced in a new environment. Dr. Neuman commented that Ravi Shankar has ceased to be taken seriously in some quarters in India because of the amount of time he spends concertizing in the United States. Time was when it was important for an Indian musician to have a foreign reputation in order to be legitimized in India. Now prolonged absences from home contribute to the tensions in the modern music scene in India.

Indian film music has influenced the semi-classical tradition of Indian music, such as *ghazal*-singing. But *filmi geet* do not seem to have had much impact in the United States. Brian Silver said that Indian classical music has had a significant effect on American composers, from Henry

Cowell in the 1930s to John Cage and Lou Harrison, and more recently Steve Reich, Terry Riley and Philip Glass, all of whom have made explicit and sensitive use of Indian musical motifs, in their ideas if not always in their actual compositions. Similarly for jazz. At a seminar on Indian influences on American music convened in Canada by Jon Higgins, David Reck reportedly commented that he thought it inconceivable that any serious North American jazz musician had not been exposed to Ravi Shankar.

Alice Kniskern expressed LC's gratitude for the assistance provided by the Archive and Research Centre for Ethnomusicology in Delhi in selecting music for participants in LC's South Asian acquisitions program. Dr. Neuman responded that it makes it much easier for the Centre to have LC purchase recordings for it, so the arrangement is a reciprocally beneficial one.

NOTES

1. *The Rags of North Indian Music: Their Structure and Evolution* (Middletown, Wesleyan University Press).
2. I believe he had three commercial recordings on HMV published in India.
3. Ragamala, incidentally, publishes *Bansri*, a journal devoted to Indian music.
4. She later finished a Master's degree at the University of Hawaii and is currently doing her Ph.D. at the University of Washington.
5. *The Tabla in Perspective* (Ann Arbor, University Microfilms, 1974).
6. *The Mridanga: A Study of Drumming in South India* (Ann Arbor: University Microfilms, 1965).
7. "India's Music," in Joseph W. Elder, ed., *Indian Civilization*, vol. II (Dubuque: Kendall/Hunt Publishing Co., 1970).
8. *Khyal: Creativity Within North India's Classical Music Tradition* (Cambridge, Eng.: Cambridge University Press, 1984).
9. *Sound, Context and Meaning in the Qawwali* (Cambridge, Eng.: Cambridge University Press, 1987). Both Wade's and Qureshi's books have been published in the recently established Cambridge Series in Ethnomusicology.
10. *The Music of the Bauls of Bengal* (Kent: Kent State University Press, 1986)
11. *Patrons and Performers in Rajasthan: The Subtle Tradition* (Delhi: Chanakya Publications, 1985).
12. In a personal communication with Ravi Shankar in 1987.
13. Just a week before these words were written in their final form, J.C. Penney's called to inquire where they might locate performing groups for each of their eight stores in the Seattle area to celebrate their India theme beginning in May 1988.

Indian Literatures in the U.S. 1957-1987

A.K. Ramanujan

It is not easy to separate American studies of Indian literatures from studies elsewhere. But, for the purposes of this paper, we shall bracket non-U.S. work on the subject.

Thirty years ago, only Sanskrit was being taught in a small number of universities and there were no area centers nor departments devoted entirely to the study of South Asia, as there are now. And this quarter-century has seen a slow expansion of our very idea of Indian civilization and of Indian literatures.

Strange things contribute to the study of a culture. When the Russians launched their Sputnik, I am sure they did not suspect that they would also launch the study of Indian languages in America. As you know, the National Defense Education Act was a direct consequence of the American feeling that they had not done as much for science and for foreign language studies as the Russians had done, and that they had not done much to stem the rising tide of Communism in the Third World. It was in 1957 that Sputnik was launched and it was in 1958 that the NDEA was passed. The Congressional Record makes the connection between the two events quite clear.

1957 was an important year for other reasons as well. It was the year that the Association for Asian Studies became full-fledged, and that was the year the Library Resources Committee was established. Maureen Patterson's unpublished essay on American studies of India over the last forty years has researched the subject with characteristic thoroughness.

Let me begin with some of the biasses that have affected our study of Indian literatures. Apart from the NDEA itself, which funded the operations, there were other interests that led our studies to take certain directions. For instance, studies of Indian languages and literatures began with philology, of which W. Norman Brown was a superb exemplar. Then, beginning with the late 1940s, came the linguists.

Many of us may not know that a great many scholars of my generation who studied Indian languages and later came to teach them and become influential in language and area centers, came from a single training program for linguistics funded by the Rockefeller Foundation, with its Indian center in Poona, from 1954 to 1959. I can think of at least fifteen such people (mostly American scholars and a small number of Indians like myself) now in this country, and an equal number in India, involved in teaching, research and policy-making in South Asian linguistics and Indian studies today.[1]

Another bias, religion, has led people, not only in America, to the study of India and its literatures. Religion is still one of the attractions of India and its literature to non-Indians. But one might also characterize it as a distraction that seduces one away from the study of Indian literatures for themselves and not as repositories of religious truths.

Linguistics, too, built a deep bias into the study, or should we say against the study of Indian literatures. For many of the linguists, both Indian and American, either didn't bring to their studies any knowledge of literature, or were innocent of any such knowledge, with a few but important exceptions. I remember my first meeting with my first American professor of linguistics. He asked me why I wanted to study linguistics. Among other things, I said I was interested in the language of literature, and he promptly responded, "Oh, literature; literature bores me." And I could see in the next few weeks that he was telling the truth: it did bore him. But he was a superb teacher of linguistics and initiated my generation to the subject through a popular textbook and his courses.

Still, the most important thing that has happened in America in the last twenty-five years in the field of Indian literatures has been, I think, the translations. I shall simply list them here as a way of remembering and recognizing these translators who have enlarged our knowledge and our view of what is Indian and what literature is in India.

For Sanskrit: Ingall's *An Anthology of Sanskrit Court Poetry*, a translation of Vidyakara's *Subhāṣitaratnakośa* of the eleventh century, with a superb introduction, and headnotes and endnotes that are often elegant little essays indispensable to any student of classical Indian poetry;[2] J.A.B. van Buitenen's monumental *Mahābhārata*, cut off in the middle, after three volumes, by his untimely death; the erudite translations of the *Rāmāyaṇa* by Robert Goldman, Sheldon Pollack et al., of which two volumes have already appeared; Barbara Miller's elegant verse translations, *Bhartṛhari*, the popular *Gītā* in a successful commercial paperback, and the three plays of Kālidāsa that she, Edwin Gerow and David Gitomer have ably translated with valuable introductions; and Wendy O'Flaherty's *Ṛgveda* and *Hindu Myths* in widely distributed Penguin Classics editions.

Hank Heifetz's verse translation of Kālidāsa's difficult *Kumārasambhava*, *The Origin of the Young God*, is excellent even though the author says so himself. C.V. Narasimhan's serviceable abridgement of the *Mahābhārata* (published by Columbia) and William Buck's rather Baroque retellings of the two epics are widely used in classes.

In Dravidian languages, Tamil is better represented than any of the other three. George L. Hart's *Poets of the Tamil Anthologies* and his path-breaking scholarly book, *The Poems of Ancient Tamil*, my own *The Interior Landscape* and *Poems of Love and War*, and David Ludden and M. Shanmukam Pillai's *Kuṟuntokai* together represent in translation almost a fourth of the classical Tamil corpus of short lyrics. For a later period of Tamil, the literature of *bhakti* has been translated by Norman Cutler in *Songs of Experience* with an original and substantial introduction to the rhetoric of *bhakti* in both Śaiva and Vaiṣṇava poetry, and by myself in *Hymns of the Drowning*, which introduces some ninety poems of the Vaiṣṇava poet Nammalvar. With the forthcoming verse translations of Cuntarar by David Shulman, and of four Śaiva saints by Indira Peterson, the Śaiva poets of Tamil *bhakti* will begin to be represented adequately.

For Kannada, my translations of four Vīraśaiva saints in the Penguin Classics, *Speaking of Śiva*, and a modern novel by Ananthamurthy, *Saṃskāra*, may be mentioned.

Telugu, which had been woefully neglected, is beginning to be represented by the translation of a folk epic, *Palnāṭu Vīracaritramu* by Gene Roghair, and a translation of Durjhaṭi's *Kāḷahastīśvarasatakamu* in *To the Lord of the Elephants* by Hank Heifetz and Narayana Rao. Narayana Rao's forthcoming translation of *Basavapurāṇa*, a Telugu compendium of Vīraśaiva saints' lives, would add much to our knowledge of *bhakti* as well as of Telugu literature.

For north India, only Hindi and Bengali have been quarried by American translators: Edward Dimock's *In Praise of Krishna*, Vaisnava poems translated into moving verse with American poet Denise Levertov, his delightful translations of courtly and village tales from Bengal in his *Thief of Love*, his long-awaited and forthcoming translation of the *bhakti* classic *Śri Caitanyacaritāmṛta*, as well as Clinton B. Seely's *With Grace and Mercy in Her Wild Hair*, Rāmprasād Sen's poems in many moods addressed to the goddess, with American poet Leonard Nathan. Tagore's *The Broken Nest* was translated by Mary Lago and Supriya Sen; *The Housewarming and Other Stories* by Mary Lago, Tarun Gupta and Amiya Chakravarthy. The somewhat truncated translation of Bibhutibhushan Banerji's *Pather Panchali* (the subject of Satyajit Ray's movie) was done in England by

T.W. Clark and Tarapada Mukerji, but was reprinted in America. Clinton Seely's forthcoming study and translations of the Bengali poet, Jibananda Das, would be among the first full-length studies of a modern Indian poet by an American—like the earlier study by Karine Schomer of the Hindi woman poet, Mahadevi Varma.

For Hindi, Linda Hess's *The Bijak of Kabir* with Shukdev Singh and Kenneth Bryant's translations of Sūrdās in *Poems to a Child God* are vivid translations of two of the most important *bhakti* poets of Hindi. Bryant and Hawley's forthcoming scholarly edition and translations of Sūrdās for the Harvard Oriental Series will inaugurate a new phase both in that series and for Hindi scholarship. For the modern period, Gordon Roadarmel's *Godan, or the Gift of a Cow* and his *A Death in the City* (short stories) were path-breakers in the 1960s. David Rubin's translations of Premchand and the poetry of Nirala are worth noting for their lucid renderings. A California project that attempted a volume of modern Hindi poetry with American poets reworking prose cribs was laudable but disappointing in results. So was a similar New York project for the Urdu *ghazals* of Ghalib, which still await an adequate translator. Robert Bly's free translations of Kabīr and Mīrā Bāī read beautifully (and even sing when he recites them) but are nowhere near the originals in structure or texture. But one is still grateful for an American poet's sympathetic recreation of them in a contemporary idiom.

For Urdu, Leslie Flemming's book on Maṇṭo stories (alas, no translations of this moving writer yet) and Naomi Lazard's translation with the poet of Faiz's important poems are notable, but not much else is available of that rich heritage.

Apart from the introductions and afterwards to these translations, few book-length works on Indian literary texts have appeared. *The Literatures of India*, by Edward Dimock et al., however unsatisfactory, especially on the modern period, is the only general introduction to the major texts so far available. Alphonso-Karkala's *Anthology of Indian Literature* is mostly unusable: it reprints dated Victorian translations (e.g., Dutt's *Rāmāyaṇa* in rhymed couplets) indiscriminately with a few modern ones. We still need a usable, critically and tastefully edited anthology of Indian literatures that represents the major genres and poets in readable contemporary translations.

In the field of literary criticism, George Hart's *Poems of Ancient India*, Alf Hiltebeitel's *The Ritual of Battle* on the *Mahabharata*, Karine Schomer's *Mahadevi Varma* and Clinton Seely on Jibananda Das, David Shulman's *The King and the Clown in South Indian Myth and Poetry*, Lee

Siegel's *Laughing Matters* on the Indian comic tradition, Edwin Gerow's *A Glossary of Indian Poetic Figures* and *Classical Sanskrit Poetics*, Annemarie Schimmel's books on Ghalib and two 18th century poets (in Urdu and Sindhi), and the American contributions to J. Gonda's many-volumed *History of Indian Literature* (Hart, Gerow, Peter Gaeffke, Annemarie Schimmel and Ludo Rocher) are notable exceptions. Edward Dimock's forthcoming book of collected essays, *The Silent Guns*, would be a welcome addition to our meager stock of literary criticism. I have omitted here the many fine works on Indian mythology whose emphases are non-literary.

Compared with Chinese or Japanese, or any of the major European literatures, one might say that few American poets have been engaged deeply enough in a serious study of Indian literatures to translate any of it directly from the original languages. They have contributed little to our studies and we have contributed very little to them. There certainly has been no Arthur Waley or Ezra Pound, as there was for Chinese, nor even a scholar like Donald Keene who, over a lifetime, made Japanese literature available and popular. Yet, as I said earlier, where there have been collaborations, as in the case of Bengali, between a scholar and a poet (Dimock and Levertov, Seely and Nathan), and in the case of Sanskrit (Masson and Merwin), the results have been happy. Of the four poets who have been interested in Indian poetry, Robert Bly, Leonard Nathan, W.S. Merwin and David Ray, only Nathan has any knowledge of an Indian language (Sanskrit).

Harvard, Chicago, California and Columbia have regularly published translations of Indian works in these decades. Of these, the Harvard Oriental Series is the oldest, and till recently contemplated only Sanskrit and Prakrit literatures. Oxford University Press, Penguin Books and other presses that have branches in America have also published Indian works, as occasionally have presses like Indiana and Yale, too.

There is only one journal devoted to South Asian literature in the country: the *Journal of South Asian Literature*, edited by Carlo Coppola, originally started by C.M. Naim and Carlo Coppola as *Mahfil*, is still going, not strong, but still alive. C.M. Naim's new journal (since 1981), *Annaal of Urdu Studies*, is the only journal devoted to a single Indian literature and it is exemplary. These journals are not well-supported by individual subscribers as they ought to be. The two major journals devoted to Asian humanities, the *Journal of the American Oriental Society* and the *Journal of Asian Studies*, publish reviews and articles of interest to students of Indian literatures, but are not particularly focused on literary concerns. Several American literary journals have run special issues devoted to Indian literatures, e.g. *Tri-Quarterly*, *Denver Review*, and *Chelsea Review*.

Now for some remarks on what has not yet happened in the field and what we would like to see happen.

Even in universities like Chicago, Columbia, California (Berkeley) or Pennsylvania, where a number of scholars are working on Indian literary texts, departments of comparative literature ignore them. Eurocentric and ethnocentric, they belie the catholicity of the term "comparative literature," to the loss of both the comparativists and the Indianists. This neglect is matched often by Indianists who do not relate creatively to the heritage of European theories and practices except in unconscious, i.e. unexamined, ways. Few relate Indian texts to comparable works elsewhere. For instance, a central text like the *Mahābhārata* has yet to be read in the context of other epics both within India and outside India: Tamil epics, oral epics in the mother tongue as well as Homer's two epics, the Bible, etc. Only Alf Hiltebeitel, both in his own work and in his translations from Dumezil, has related other Indo-European traditions to the Indian epic, though somewhat narrowly in terms set by Dumezil; his forthcoming work on the South Indian Draupadi cults and folk traditions that reinterpret and contemporize the epic story and characters in living ritual, song and performance, promises to break new ground. Some stirrings in this comparative direction are also felt in the courses given at California (Berkeley), Columbia and Chicago.

I believe that Americans studying Indian literatures should be grounded deeply in their own literature, for a true sensibility cannot be acquired except in one's mother tongue, where one doesn't have to look up dictionaries and grammars to understand a text. For in a mother tongue, the reader of literature has ready access to unspoken and life-long associations as one does not in a foreign language. Taste and judgement, difficult and precarious in any tradition, even in one's mother tongue, are more firmly rooted when based on mother-tongue literatures. Otherwise, one is intimidated by the foreign texts, overvalues minor texts because one has invested enormous time and effort in deciphering them, or one becomes timidly positivistic or philological instead of being imaginative and interpretative. I think the real paucity of original interpretations of Indian literatures in American work stems from this lack as much as any other.

Hence, too, the bias toward reading literature as document, as anthropology, rather than as art; culling the obvious fact rather than sensing the subtle knot of form and content that literature is. One is reminded of the Sanskrit saying about the lover who, while loosening the knot of his woman's skirt, can only think of the price of the skirt.[3] A great deal of Indian literature is read not because it is literature but because it is Indian—to diagnose India, to illustrate social science or religious concerns. We forget that what is content to others is form to the artist.

The whole of culture, every element in it, whether it is kinship or kingship, religious belief and custom, male-female relations, and so on, is background and material out of which the arts arise—always ringing changes on them in ways that will be entirely missed if the literariness of the literary text, its specific density, is not grasped with both sides of one's brain. It is being read, by and large, by the right brain alone to extract facts, illustrate ideas. If I may exaggerate to make the point, it is read mostly not for pleasure or even for pain, but only for immediate "profit." But pleasure and pain in the detail of art works are the royal roads to art experience.

A similar lack of interest also extends to contemporary Indian literatures. We seem to have left contemporary India mostly to social, particularly to political, scientists. Our literary scholars are rarely interested in it. One not grounded in one's own literature, in one's own contemporary literature as well, is unsure or contemptuous or uncritical of contemporary Indian work. Translators in the U.S., for instance, rarely translate contemporary Indian poems or novels. Hardly two or three good novels from India have been translated and published in this country in the past twenty-five years.

But the situation will change if, in our education of American students of Indian literatures, we could (a) begin with an acquaintance with the literary masterpieces of Europe, England and America; (b) cultivate the reading of Indian texts in the original not at a snail's pace, with dictionaries and grammars, but at the pace for which they are written (for literary experience is a matter of pace as well as of slowing down), aiming at a command of the languages we rarely aim at; (c) use a comparative perspective which is inevitably contrastive, individuating both the English texts and the Indian ones by the perception of contrasts among the commonalities; d) deal with them as live, not as dead, texts, relating them to contemporary perspectives and literary practice.

Lastly, we need to remember the influential, ever-present oral traditions that surround every Indian text. The relevance of folklore to all our Indianist disciplines cannot be overly stressed, especially as a counterweight to the weight of Sanskritism and textualism. A small band of scholars, mostly social scientists, are beginning to attend to folk literature: the work of

Peter Claus on the Tulu *pāḍdanas*, Brenda Beck's *The Epic of the Three Twins* on a Tamil oral epic, Blackburn's forthcoming translations of the Tamil Bow Songs or *villuppāṭṭus*, the collection *Folktales of India*, edited by Beck, Claus, et al., Roghair's Telugu oral epic in translation, *Palnāṭu Vīracaritramu*, the new essays in *Another Harmony*, edited by Blackburn and Ramanujan and a forthcoming collection of essays on Indian oral epics by Blackburn, Wadley, et al. are worth mentioning.

Our very best work done so far, in spite of everything I have said, small though it is, already fulfills these criteria. Indeed, these criteria are drawn from them. A knowledge of the kind and quality envisaged here of Indian languages and literatures will deepen all our disciplines, bring fresh insights and make possible the emergence of new paradigms for the study of Indian civilization. If that happens in the next twenty-five years, with luck, we would have the luxury of an entirely new set of complaints.

DISCUSSION

Dr. Hart commented that one of the major problems in dealing with the classical tradition is that the classical aestheticians themselves do not analyze works as a whole but as a series of parts. Too often it has become standard practice to excerpt a segment from a text and treat is as a separate whole rather than as a part of something larger. You sometimes wonder what the connection is between the poem and the commentator. Dr. Hart recommended Hank Heifetz's unpublished thesis as a controversial but often valuable discussion of the problems of translation. The speaker agreed that one cannot take the commentators on faith. He said we must take a third position which is neither that of the poet nor the commentators but one that comes from our cultivation of our own sensibilities. To understand a poem fully, we must respond to it not so much intellectually but in the ways that one sensibility takes a position toward another. It is this literary sensibility that also makes people like Clifford Geertz fine social scientists who can produce ideas on which a great many people feed. Their imaginations work not only on the facts but through a certain position towards them.

Dr. Rudolph noted that Americans tend to view India through the lenses of their own constructs. Some regard the Ramayan as a dreadfully anti-feminist text. You've got to get them beyond that. Raman's speaking about humor and the Indian aesthetic vision complements rather than conflicts with social science approaches. The humanist tends to relate to the individual and the social scientist to the group. Both have a role to play in the difficult task of conveying a sense of the whole of a network of cultural attitudes as complex and different as those of India.

NOTES

1. M.L. Apte (Marathi, Hindi: Duke University); K.C. Bahl (Hindi, Panjabi: Chicago); William Bright (Kannada, Hindi: UCLA); George Cardona (Gujarati: Pennsylvania); E.C. Dimock (Bengali: Chicago); Paul Friedrich (Malayalam: Chicago); John Gumperz (Hindi: Berkeley, California); William McCormack (Kannada: Calgary); C.M. Naim (Urdu, Hindi: Chicago); A.K. Ramanujan (Tamil, Kannada: Chicago); Norman Zide (Hindi, Mundari: Chicago); Gerald Kelley (Telugu: Cornell); Franklin Southworth (Marathi, Hindi: Pennsylvania); Paul Staneslaw (Hindi, Gujarati: Minnesota); R. Radhakrishnan (Tamil: Calgary) are among the alumni of that program who have prepared either grammars or teaching materials and are still active in India programs. One could make a similar list for India.
2. For bibliographic details, see the bibliography below.
3. I am indebted to George Hart for this saying.

BIBLIOGRAPHY

For a comprehensive bibliography of Indian literatures (till 1980), consult the Languages and Literatures sections of Maureen L.P. Patterson's *South Asian Civilizations: A Bibliographic Synthesis* (Chicago and London: University of Chicago Press, 1981). In the following list, articles and books forthcoming are not included, although they were mentioned in the text.

Alphonso-Karkala, John B. *An Anthology of Indian Literature*. (2nd rev. edn.) Delhi: Indian Council for Cultural Relations, 1987.

Anantha Murthy, U.R. *Samskara*: *A Rite for a Dead Man*. (Transl. from Kannada by A.K. Ramanujan) Delhi: Oxford Univ. Press, 1978.

Archer, William G. *Songs for the Bride: Wedding Rites of Rural India*. (Ed. by Barbara Stoler Miller and Mildred Archer) NY: Columbia Univ. Press, 1986.

Banerji, Bibhutibhushan. *Pather Panchali* (*Song of the Road*). (Transl. from Bengali by T.W. Clark and Tarapada Mukerji) Bloomington: Indian Univ. Press, 1968.

Beck, Brenda E.F. et al. *Folktales of India*. (Ed. by Brenda E.F. Beck with a foreword by A.K. Ramanujan) Chicago: Univ. of Chicago Press, 1987.

——. *The Three Twins: The Telling of a South Indian Folk Epic*. Bloomington: Indiana Univ. Press, 1982.

Bhagavadgītā. *The Bhagavadgītā: Krishna's Counsel in Time of War*. (Transl. by Barbara Stoler Miller) Toronto and NY: Bantam Books, 1986.

Bhartṛhari. *Bhartṛhari: Poems*. (Transl. by Barbara Stoler Miller) NY: Columbia Univ. Press, 1967.

Blackburn, Stuart H. and A.K. Ramanujan, eds. *Another Harmony: New Essays on the Folklore of India*. Berkeley: Univ. of California Press, 1986.

Bryant, Kenneth E. *Poems to the Child-God: Structures and Strategies in the Poetry of Surdas*. Berkeley: Univ. of California Press, 1978.

Buck, William. *Rāmāyaṇa: King Rama's Way*. Berkeley: Univ. of California Press, 1973

——. *Mahābhārata*. Berkeley: Univ. of California Press, 1973.

Cutler, Norman. *Songs of Experience: The Poetics of Tamil Devotion*. Bloomington: Indiana Univ. Press, 1987.

Dhurjati. *For the Lord of the Animals: Poems from the Telugu: The Kalahastisvara Satakamu of Dhurjati*. (Transl. with an introduction and notes by Hank Heifetz and Velcheru Narayana Rao) Berkeley: Univ. of California Press, 1987.

Dimock, Edward C., Jr., et al. *The Literatures of India: An Introduction*. Chicago: Univ. of Chicago Press, 1974.

——. *The Place of the Hidden Moon: Erotic Mysticism in the Vaiṣṇavasahajiya Cult of Bengal*. Chicago: Univ. of Chicago Press, 1974.

——, ed. and transl. *The Thief of Love: Bengali Tales from Court and Village*. Chicago: Univ. of Chicago Press, 1963.

Faiz, Faiz Ahmad. *The True Subject: Selected Poems of Faiz Ahmad Faiz*. (Transl. by Naomi Lazard) Princeton, NJ: Princeton Univ. Press, 1988.

Flemming, Leslie A. *Another Lonely Voice: The Urdu Short Stories of Saadat Hasan Manto*. Berkeley: Center for South and Southeast Asian Studies, #18, Univ. of California, 1979.

Gerow, Edwin. *A Glossary of Indian Figures of Speech*. The Hague: Mouton, 1971.

——. *Indian Poetics*. Wiesbaden: Harrassowitz, 1977.

Hart, George L., III. *The Poems of Ancient Tamil: Their Milieu and Their Sanskrit Counterparts*. Berkeley: Univ. of California Press, 1975.

Hiltebeitel, Alf. *The Ritual of Battle: Krishna in the Mahābhārata*. Ithaca, NY: Cornell Univ. Press, 1976.

Hindu Myths: A Sourcebook. (Transl. from Sanskrit with an introduction by Wendy Doniger O'Flaherty) Harmondsworth and Baltimore: Penguin Books, 1975.

In Praise of Krishna: Songs from the Bengali. (Transl. by Edward C. Dimock, Jr. and Denise Levertov. With an introduction and notes by Edward C. Dimock, Jr.) Chicago: Univ. of Chicago Press, 1967, 1981.

Kabīr. *The Bijak of Kabir*. (Transl. by Linda Hess and Shukdev Singh. With essays and notes by Linda Hess) San Francisco: North Point Press, 1983.

Kālīdasa. *The Origin of the Young God: Kālīdasa's Kumārasambhava*. (Translated with annotations and an introduction by Hank Heifetz) Berkeley: Univ. of California Press, 1985.

——. *Theater of Memory: The Plays of Kālīdasa*. (Ed. by Barbara Stoler Miller. Translated by the editor, Edwin Gerow and David Gitomer) NY: Columbia Univ. Press, 1984.

Kuruntokai. *The Interior Landscape*. (Poems selected and transl. by A.K. Ramanujan) Bloomington: Indiana Univ. Press, 1967; paperback edn., 1975.

Kuṟuntokai: An Anthology of Classical Tamil Love Poetry. (Transl. by M. Shanmugam Pillai and David E. Ludden) Madurai, India: Koodal Publishers, 1976.

Lago, Mary M. *Rabindranath Tagore*. Boston: Twayne Publishers, 1976.

Mahābhārata. The Mahābhārata. (Transl. with an introd. and notes by J.A,B. van Buitenen) 3 vols. Chicago: Univ. of Chicago Press, 1973.

Modern Hindi Short Stories. (Transl. by Gordon Roadarmel) Berkeley: Univ. of California Press, 1974. (First pub. in 1972 under title: *A Death in Delhi*).

Nammāḻvār. *Hymns for the Drowning: Poems for Viṣṇu*. (Transl. from Tamil by A.K. Ramanujan) Princeton, NJ: Princeton Univ. Press, 1981.

Narasimhan, C.V. *The Mahabharata*. NY: Columbia Univ. Press, 1965.

Nirala. *A Season on the Earth: Selected Poems of Nirala*. (Transl. by David Rubin) NY: Columbia Univ. Press, 1976.

Poems of Love and War: From the Eight Anthologies and the Ten Long Poems of Classical Tamil. (Selected and transl. by A.K. Ramanujan) NY: Columbia Univ. Press, 1985.

Poems of the Tamil Anthologies: Ancient Poems of Love and War. (Transl. by George L. Hart, III) Princeton, NJ: Princeton Univ. Press, 1979.

Premchand. *The Gift of a Cow: A Translation of the Hindi Novel Godan*. (Transl. by Gordon Roadarmel) Bloomington: Indiana Univ. Press, 1968.

——. *The World of Premchand: Short Stories by Premchand*. (Transl. by David Rubin) Bloomington: Indiana Univ. Press, 1969.

Ramanujan, A.K., comp. *Speaking of Śiva*. (Transl. with an introd. by A.K. Ramanujan) Harmondsworth: Penguin Books, 1973.

Rāmprāsad Sen. *With Grace and Mercy in Her Wild Hair: Selected Poems to the Mother Goddess*. (Transl. by Leonard Nathan and Clinton Seely) Boulder: Great Eastern, 1982.

Ṛgveda. The Rig Veda: An Anthology of One Hundred and Eight Hymns. (Selected, annotated and transl. by Wendy Doniger O'Flaherty) Harmondsworth and NY: Penguin Books, 1981.

Roghair, Gene. *The Epic of Palnadu: A Study and Translation of Palnati Virula Katha, a Telugu Oral Tradition from Andhra Pradesh, India*. NY: Oxford Univ. Press, 1982.

Sanskrit Love Poetry. (Transl. by W. S. Merwin and J. Moussaieff Masson. With an introd. by J. Moussaieff Masson) NY: Columbia Univ. Press, 1977.

Schimmel, Annemarie. *Pain and Grace: A Study of Two Mystical Writers of Eighteenth Century Muslim India*. Leiden: Brill, 1976.

——. *Sindhi Literature*. Wiesbaden: Harrassowitz, 1974. (History of Indian Literature, 8:4)

Schomer, Karine. *Mahadevi Varma and the Chhayavad Age of Modern Hindi Poetry*. Berkeley: Univ. of California Press, 1983.

Shulman, David Dean. *The King and the Clown in South Indian Myth and Poetry*. Princeton, NJ: Princeton Univ. Press, 1985.

Siegel, Lee. *Laughing Matters: Comic Tradition in India*. Chicago: Univ. of Chicago Press, 1987.

Tagore, Rabindranath. *The Broken Nest* (*Nashtanir*). (Transl. by Mary M. Lago and Supriya Sen. With an introd. by Mary M. Lago) Columbia, MO: Univ. of Missouri Press, 1971.

——. *Housewarming and Other Selected Writings*. (Ed. with an introd. by Amiya Chakravarty; transl. by Mary M. Lago, Tarun Gupta and the editor) NY: New American Library, 1965.

Vālmīki. *The Rāmāyaṇa* (*Ayodhyākaṇḍa*). (Transl. with an introd. and notes by Sheldon I. Pollock) Princeton, NJ: Princeton Univ. Press, 1986.

——. *The Rāmāyaṇa* (*Bālakaṇḍa*). (Transl. with an introd. and notes by Robert P. Goldman) Princeton, NJ: Princeton Univ. Press, 1984.

Vidyakara, comp. *An anthology of Sanskrit Court Poetry*. (Transl. with an introd. and notes by Daniel H.H. Ingalls) Cambridge, MA: Harvard Univ. Press, 1965.

American Understanding of Indian Culture: The Festival of India

Ted M.G. Tanen

Those of us who have been involved, either as scholars or administrators, in the basic task of increasing American understanding of India, have long been aware of the difficulty of communicating our own insights and appreciation to others. There has been tremendous interchange in the last few decades between American and Indian scholars in many fields, and the value and benefits of this process have been amply demonstrated in the discussions of the last few days. There has also been a good deal of communication between American and Indian non-academic specialists in the professions and in various scientific and technical fields. All of this has resulted in a strong network of institutional and individual links between the two countries, and in ever-expanding circles of American professionals in many fields who are working in India, collaborating on joint projects with Indian colleagues, and in general increasing and strengthening our understanding of India.

When we move outside these professional circles, however, and into the vast majority of our population who have neither jobs nor personal resources permitting direct contacts with far-away countries, the misperceptions of India, and the general lack of interest in correcting these misperceptions, are immense.

For this reason, to the Subcommission the concept of a Festival of India presented a new and extremely exciting opportunity. We saw it as an experiment, as a challenge, as an opportunity to make it possible for thousands—perhaps millions—of Americans to have a first-hand encounter with Indian culture. We also saw it as an important step in the on-going process of cultural exchange in which the Subcommission and many other organizations have been active participants, and hopefully as a step that would explore new paths and open new opportunities for us all.

To my mind, the goals of cultural exchange are very basic. There are countries in the world, such as India, which are major cultural and political entities, but which have been ignored and misunderstood by Americans, including Americans at the highest levels of political power. The United

States as a world power cannot afford to ignore nor to misunderstand a country such as India, and Americans, as citizens of the world, should not be ignorant of the cultural orientations of such a major world civilization. There are responsibilities which go along with being a world power, as well as with being a citizen of such a power. This, of course, was Senator Fulbright's basic philosophy.

Those of us who are involved in international cultural exchange have long recognized the unique power that artistic expressions have to communicate across political and other barriers, and the special potential of what is increasingly being referred to as "cultural diplomacy." A single performance or work of art can have an impact on its audience; concentrating events and exhibitions into a coordinated cultural "festival" increases the impact profoundly. A Festival of India, in and of itself, may not change conceptions and misconceptions. What it does do, however, is provide us with a method of capturing the attention of a large audience, at least for a short time. Once the attention is caught, it is then up to us—those of us who spend our professional lives engaged in this task of "increasing international understanding"—to figure out how to hold onto the attention of this new audience, and how to turn momentary curiosity into lasting and thoughtful interest and appreciation.

Before we can work out the most effective means to follow up the Festival of India, we must be clear about what such festivals actually accomplish. As many of you already know, the American Secretariat of the Subcommission is looking into this very question, and at the moment we are compiling a modest, in-house study of the tangible results and impact of the Festival on American audiences. This work is still in process, but already much can be said.

The Festival of India encompassed events ranging from spectacular exhibitions at this country's most respected museums to single lectures and performances arranged by local community groups. It included performances of traditional and contemporary Indian music, dance and theater at major arts institutions and at universities and performance spaces throughout the country; more than one hundred exhibitions at major museums as well as at colleges, libraries, galleries and regional and specialized museums; poetry readings; film festivals; public affairs programs; and a dazzling Indian *mela* on the Mall in Washington, D.C., which drew over one million people. More than one dozen books and exhibition catalogs have been published, and hundreds of articles and magazine stories have resulted. Publicity on the Festival has just passed the one billion audience mark, meaning that the combined print and broadcast viewer figures show that, theoretically, every American could have heard something about the Festival several times over.

Some of you may know that the Festival also included eighteen major conferences and symposia, in which more than one hundred distinguished Indian scholars, artists, journalists, scientists, government officials and others took part. More than half of these visitors remained in the States for periods ranging from a few days to several months, giving lectures and taking part in other Festival programs.

So far, we have documented close to 700 separate events and activities taking place in towns, cities and villages in 43 states. And a large majority of these events were totally spontaneous: events that were organized independently and autonomously, inspired by the Festival of India but not in any way connected with any "official" Festival body.

What does all this mean? And what have the actual results been? Some results of the Festival can be identified and documented. By the time our in-house study is completed, we will know approximately how many Americans attended Festival events; how many American funding agencies, academic institutions and arts organizations took part; how many of these were demonstrating a new interest in India, and how many of them plan to maintain this interest. We will know how many books and articles were published and what their estimated circulation will be. We will have a fairly accurate idea of how much the Festival cost and we will be able to break down where the contributions came from. Already we know that tourism in India has increased and that everyone, from Government of India officials to travel agents and tour operators, credits the Festival with at least a good part of this increase. We know that there are new markets for high-quality Indian imports, and that at least some of this is directly related to Festival activities. We know that the chief art critic of the *New York Times* filled the front cover of the *Sunday Times Magazine* and the front page of the *Sunday Arts* section with articles on and illustrations of Festival exhibitions, and pointed to the Festival as one of the major cultural events of the year. We know that there are films, television programs, books and exhibitions planned because of the Festival. We know that in many cities, Americans of Indian descent or background became involved with local cultural organizations for the first time during the Festival, and that, in many cases, this is leading to on-going future collaborative plans.

These things and others can be directly attributed to the Festival. There are also signs of many other positive things happening, such as increased interest in India-related courses at colleges and universities, and increased U.S.-Indo business collaboration, which are probably due primarily to other factors. The Festival of India benefitted greatly from the timeliness of its appearance. The number of popular films and television shows being released on India; the emergence of a new Prime Minister who has opened new opportunities for commercial relationships; the growing numbers of Indians occupying highly visible professional positions in this country; even the crises and tragedies which have besieged India during the last few years; all of these have served to put India in the minds of Americans, and helped make them receptive to the Festival of India.

We hope that the Festival of India has played a useful part in the process of increasing understanding. In the hundreds of interviews that we have conducted (and are continuing to conduct) with people who were involved in Festival activities, the one word that comes up in almost every single case is "awareness." Awareness is not something that can be measured or quantified, but people who took part in almost every aspect of the Festival seem to agree that awareness of India has increased as a result. What happens next, of course, is most important.

The Festival of India was a collaborative venture organized by two governments, their designated coordinating bodies and an extremely large number of arts institutions and academic, cultural and funding organizations, backed up by the creative contributions of scholars, specialists, administrators, Americans from India and Americans interested in India. Whatever success the Festival has achieved can be attributed to the diversity and energy of these many contributors and organizers. In developing ways to follow up the momentum and to strengthen and increase the interest, this same diversity and energy is essential, and we hope that all those who so willingly took part in making the Festival of India happen will work with us in planning for the more permanent results.

I hope that this symposium will help us, not only in assessing past and current levels of understanding of India, but also in serving as a starting point for all of us as we begin developing new ways to collaborate and cooperate in the future.

DISCUSSION

The speaker said that the Festival had been widely publicized in India. There have been 13 programs done by Bombay television on exhibits and seminars in the U.S., all of them good and some extraordinary, and a number of articles in national magazines. However, there has also been a good deal of negative publicity in India. To anyone familiar with India, such a reaction would seem normal.

A major complaint was that precious Indian artifacts were being sent out of the country but Americans were not exhibiting anything of value in India in return. But there was also a fear of damage. Dr. Chandra suggested that Indian museologists are relatively inexperienced in loaning materials and may be more apprehensive than would be their Western counterparts.

Some Indians had the impression that the image of India conveyed was that of a land of bullocks and fire-walkers rather than a modern state building factories and experimenting in nuclear physics. Mr. Tanen pointed out that India's modern scientific and technological achievements were emphasized in seminars, articles and a travelling science exhibit. It is difficult to portray this type of activity in what we think of as a cultural context.

Unfortunately, the speaker said, there is no concerted effort planned to capture and extend the interest evoked by the Festival, although, of course, the various organizations already supporting Indian studies will continue.

After some further discussion of Indian misgivings, the speaker quoted a colleague as expressing the opinion that, if the Festival could be considered a contest, surely India won.

Concluding Remarks

Stanley J. Heginbotham

The first theme that emerged in our symposium was that of detachment versus engagement, which Susanne Rudolph enunciated during a discussion session and which went back and forth during the course of the symposium. A summing up sounds objective and detached; the two days of discussions, I fear, have made me very much engaged. I've had very personal reactions to what has been said and discussed and I will present to you some very personal responses in an effort to draw together some of the themes that I found particularly important.

I will speak in a distant voice: a voice that is distant from Indian studies in substance because my professional responsibilities rarely overlap with the substance of Indian studies these days, and a distant perspective and a distant voice professionally because my professional responsibilities as a manager of policy analysis, somewhat to my surprise, rarely overlap with the field of academic Indian studies.

I'd like to share with you my reflections on what was said during the course of this symposium and my surprise that some things were not said. Susanne Rudolph began by defining the quest for understanding of India in terms of two types of conflict: conflict over theory and conflict over methods. She delineated the conflict between those who took an adaptive, evolutionary view and those who saw enduring cleavages in India that could be resolved only by revolution. Among the evolutionists, she identified the conflict between those ethnocentric, structural functionalists who tried to fit India within universal categories, and those who espoused a culturally embedded modernization, which one might well identify as a Rudolphian approach. I think the conflicts go well beyond that in political science to those who challenged the very ability to use modern or modernization as a category, because it was impossible to define "modern" independent of "western," and thus it was impossible to think non-ethnocentrically of modernization.

She identified a series of methodological conflicts focusing around formalism and anti-formalism: the center/periphery conflict; the elites versus the non-elites or lesser elites conflict; the conflict between those who focused on ideology, beliefs and proclaimed reasons for behavior, versus those who focused on material interests and behavioral analysis to get at the causes of behavior; the conflict between the quantitativists and the qualitativists; the conflict between those who saw villages as isolates and those who saw them imbedded in wider cultures. It seems extraordinary to me that there should have been so many conflicts in so short a period of academic research and analysis, but on reflection, it is an extraordinarily accurate observation. George Hart, in his non-criticism of Susanne, when he said, "Well, he didn't mean it critically, but she could really have said the same thing ten years ago," hinted, I think, at a very important point, which is that these are conflicts that were very much compressed in time into the 1950s, 60s and early 70s.

We are indebted to Susanne for having identified and categorized them so nicely, but I think it reemphasizes the enormously conflictual character of the research enterprise we are engaged in. I pondered the consequences of those conflicts, some of which were very positive. We got as a result an extraordinary mapping of Indian culture and society. Each thesis and antithesis pushed researchers into new and varied areas of India, and enabled them to identify local and regional diversities and differences and levels of behavior and activity. This process has provided us with an enormously rich body of knowledge.

The negative side of it, and here I speak personally and somewhat speculatively, is that it was theoretically devastating. The introduction of broad theory is perceived as dangerous. A lot of us have been hurt badly as our theoretical constructs were attacked, and we have consequently retreated into defining works by what seems methodologically appropriate. We have reverted to a lot of mid-level theory that has seemed manageable. I personally felt a sense of caution and timidity in defining, identifying and proclaiming the significance of this vast body of knowledge.

The central conflict that reemerged time and again in the course of our discussions was the conflict between India in a comparative or universalistic perspective. Susanne raised this in the context of structural functionalism versus Rudolphian approaches. Barbara Metcalf raised it in terms of Islam seen in isolation versus Islam illuminated by its existence in competing comparative contexts. Wendy O'Flaherty raised it in the context of Hinduism as the birthplace of *homo religiosus*, proclaiming "Ouch" in Sanskrit when he first stepped on a sharp stone, rather than as a distinctive product of unique cultures and subcultures. Professor Chandra raised it in the context of his discussion of Coomaraswamy, whether art appreciation had to be internal to a culture or was subject to universal standards and perspectives. And repeatedly raised was the issue of the value of area studies versus a disciplinary perspective, inferentially always a comparative perspective.

There are three important values associated with this conflict. One is that one not lose data as a result of cross-cultural categorization. The comparativists want to dilute Indian reality by fitting that reality into cross-cultural comparisons and categories. A second value is avoiding falling prey to ethnocentric theoretical fallacies that have bedeviled many of our efforts at theoretical formulations. The third value that was discussed was that of a kind of intellectual protectionism which was provoked by Burton Stein's metaphor of Indian studies as a firm in a free market. In response, George Hart suggested that South Asian literature was like an infant industry that needed protection from the more vigorous and powerful forces of analysis applied to French and other European literatures. We also heard Professor White's moving image of himself personally, and, by extension analysis, of Hindi literature, as a stockpiled strategic resource or a refrigerated cheese waiting for an occasion when there would be demand for its distribution.

These discussions imparted a sense that the tradition we're concerned with is a battered and buffeted ship in need of protection. Some of the debate on this issue suffered from an either/or fallacy. It seems to me that we do, in fact, need both the institutions that focus particularly on India and those that treat it in various comparative perspectives. As Norman Brown was said to have noted, "Area studies are needed as units that protect and provide assurance of survival of Indian studies in a very competitive university environment." But I think it is clear also that we need the insights and the theory that derive from conceptual and comparative traditions.

Now let me say something about one of the most surprising features of the symposium. It seemed to me that there were two discussions going on here, one a discussion of American scholarship on India, and the other a discussion of American understanding of India. It was remarkably rare that the two discussions were held simultaneously. There were, I think, marvelous depictions of the sources of American understanding of India that focused on the role of merchants, of missionaries, of Indians in the American context, of monotheists responding to multitheistic, pluralistic Indian religion, of musicians, of swamis, of a whole set of sources of influence that have shaped American perceptions and understanding of India. And then there were discussions of American scholarship on India, which focused very much on our knowledge but not a lot on American understanding of India. This is partly due, I think, to the undue modesty of many of our speakers, who have in fact played significant personal roles in expanding American understanding of India through their writings, their speaking and their other activities. But I think it is also partly a result of the trauma of trying but failing to achieve the perhaps mistaken goal of a value-free set of theoretical frameworks in the context of an inadequate view of the role of comparison.

Thomas Kuhn was mentioned a number of times over the course of the discussions. Kuhn talks about paradigmatic and normal sciences. He suggests that in science there are occasions when one has blinding theoretical insights, statements, ways of thinking about data that are often totally uninformed by scientific method. These are followed by a second phase of verification of these proposed discoveries in which, with methodological rigor, detailed and repeated incremental testing is carried out to either verify, refute or refine these grand theoretical or paradigmatic statements. I suggest the importance of a third stage that Kuhn does not discuss. That is the stage of interpretation, of the diffusion of results. This, it seems to me, is the focus of the responsibility that this seminar suggests; a self-conscious pedagogy in which we, as teachers, consider how best to translate, to reflect, to interpret to a broader audience the meaning and significance of our knowledge and discoveries.

Ted Tanen spoke of the Festival of India as a vehicle for creating an awareness, a consciousness-raising, and issued the challenge to us as scholars to build upon that initial awareness. We usually think of comparativism as an instrument of discovery; as a means of helping us develop theory and insight. It is also very important to think of it as an instrument of interpretation. If you think of it in that way, comparison is evaluated not so much from the perspective of whether it is theoretically enlightening but whether it gives meaning to a particular audience; whether you can move from the detachment of the scholar to engagement, and the development of a passionate interest in what the audience perceives. Comparison can be used to engage the American values, problems and dilemmas of the individuals in an audience, and this shared, personal engagement can be linked to universal human dilemmas, problems and values.

To illustrate, consider three striking and instructive vehicles of understanding of India that, to my amazement, were never mentioned in the course of the symposium: the *Raj Quartet*, *Passage to India* and *Gandhi*. The first two, *Raj Quartet* and *Passage to India*, focus, it seems to me, on how different human beings respond to being thrust into a foreign setting that is perceived in terms of race, color, culture and inferiority in ill-defined sets of causal relationships. I think many American listeners and observers identified with the dilemmas and situations of the British in the contexts of both of these vehicles. Although we could do this from the safety of being able to distinguish ourselves from the British, the parallels with the dilemmas Americans face in dealing with blacks as well as with Third World cultures and societies are very clear. This parallel was an important aspect of our emotional involvement with those two vehicles. I don't know of anything in literature more moving than the dilemma of Hari Kumar in the *Raj Quartet*, who is at once Indian and Western, but non-white, and who experiences the reality of the clashes of cultures, the clashes of race and the clashes of perception of cultural superiority and inferiority. *Gandhi*, it seems to me, strikes at our fascination with the sources of personal authority and with a peculiar American ambivalence toward non-violence and revolution.

Our silence on these three vehicles is possibly rooted in the fact that none of them gets at what we think of as the "real" India. But their power as vehicles derives from the fact that they get at the real American. This proposition calls attention to something we mentioned very little in the symposium, the American in American understanding of India. Susanne Rudolph referred to America's predisposition to rally to support democracy in India; M.N. Srinivas referred at several points to the relevance of Indian experience to affirmative action programs in America, to problems of democracy, to ethnicity in democracy and to modernization. Barbara Metcalf referred to the power of fear of Islamic fundamentalism in shaping and attracting attention to the kinds of work she has done on Islam. Wendy O'Flaherty referred to the empathetic view of religion and the fact that it is now *declasse* to study current manifestations of Indian religion. She referred to the conflict of the benefits of a caste system with American values of egalitarianism. There were other points, including Barbara Miller's discussion of her attempts to tie the *Gita* to Thoreau and T.S. Eliot in order to engage students' interest. Professor Chandra made use of the Coomaraswamy concept of a hierarchy of understanding. The point is that Americans begin to understand India in the context of their own problems, values and dilemmas. I was struck by how much so many of you have to say about India to your students and non-scholars. As a political scientist, I am especially impressed by the value and remarkable character of the open and competitive political system of India. It seems to me as I study and try to reflect to Congress the character of political systems around the world, India has emerged as a great political miracle in the history of post-World War II politics. This is a society of such extraordinary diversity that the fact that a democratic system has been created and perpetuated that holds together as an effective, operative and meaningful system of representative politics amid such diversity is nothing short of remarkable. I think for Americans who are interested in the character of democratic process and the ways democracies work, there is an enormous amount to engage Americans in the character, the nature and the sources of success of the Indian political process.

I think one of the things India can help us do is to look at the peculiarities of our own society. Let me point out two that I think are particularly fruitful areas that again were mentioned in the course of the sessions. One is the issue of hierarchy versus egalitarianism. We think of India as at a pole, having traditionally insisted upon class and caste differences. We sometimes don't reflect on the fact that the United States is at the other end of the pole, and is far more determined and aggressive in its espousal of egalitarianism than virtually any other society in the world. What is striking to me in dealing with Indians particularly is the extent to which we are uncomfortable with hierarchy and power relations. As a bureaucrat and a manager of 75 people here at the Library, I am amused at my behavior and the extent to which I go to disguise the fact that I have power over the people who work under me, because we are not prepared to accept hierarchy. We are predisposed to not accept unequal power relations. They are necessary, I submit, in any society, and for us to deny them to the extent that we do is quite as extraordinary as the richness we discover in the extent to which Indians emphasize hierarchy. I submit that one of the major sources of tension between these two societies is the fact that we are at opposing poles in our approaches to hierarchy and equality. By emphasizing, discussing and developing these concepts, we learn about ourselves and we engage Americans in a better understanding of India. I think we also begin to see the very important changes that are taking place in India as Indians become better adapted at and skilled in dealing with egalitarian relationships and muting and softening what has often seemed to be grating behavior in a non-egalitarian system.

I would, as a second example, emphasize the difference between India as a society that has passion for the proper order of things, for avoiding conflict, for defining relationships in such a way that conflict is removed; a system that provides order, justice and the absence of conflict in contrast to the American passion for what works, for what produces results and for what manages conflict. Here I come back to what I consider the miracle of Indian democracy. It is striking to me that for many Indians, democracy as practiced in India is an embarrassment, because it is characterized by conflicts, by tensions, by ethnicity. An American looks at this system and sees remarkable achievement because we assume that there is going to be conflict; we assume there is going to be ethnicity and tension. What impresses us is the fact that it is resolved, that it is managed in ways that preserve democratic process. To us, that is a remarkable achievement. To many Indians, it is a symptom of failure. It is something they don't want us to investigate. They don't want us to observe it because it reflects a focus on what many Indians have traditionally seen as a negative feature of their society. I think this is very much at the center or focal point of the discussions we have had on visas. It characterizes, I think, a profound dilemma and tension because, from our perspective, the very ideas that put India in its greatest and best light are off-limits. It is the Government of India's sovereign right, which I do not in any way question, to deny visas or to focus or limit the research that Americans do on particular subjects. I perfectly understand from their point of view why they do so and I don't say that disparagingly or in objection, but it does seem to me a real irony that the fact that we are at poles in our notions of the value of order and balance on the one hand, and our focus on ways of getting results on the other, leads to this serious failure of mutual understanding.

It seems to me that scholarship has an opportunity to touch students with features of India that arouse elements of passion and passionate interest in India. Coomaraswamy's paradigm can be the base for building deeper layers of understanding among Americans of this rich and varied society in which we share such a strong personal and passionate interest.